Wedding Etiquette
Properly Explained

Also available in this series:

Best Man's Duties
Sample Social Speeches
The Right Joke For The Right Occasion
Babies Names A–Z
Joke after Joke after Joke
Buying Or Selling A House
A–Z Of Do-It-Yourself In The Home

Uniform with this book

Wedding Etiquette
Properly Explained

**Marriage
under all Denominations**

by
VERNON HEATON

PAPERFRONTS
**ELLIOT RIGHT WAY BOOKS
KINGSWOOD, SURREY, U.K.**

CONTENTS

ACKNOWLEDGEMENTS

The following are thanked for their information and help:
Catholic Marriage Advisory Council
Jewish Marriage Council

Deputy Registrar General – Northern Ireland
The Registrar General for Scotland
The Superintendent Registrar for Epsom

Church of Scotland
Church of Ireland
The Presbyterian Church in Ireland
The Methodist Church in Ireland
Armagh Regional Marriage Tribunal

Father Nigel Griffin, Church of the Good Shepherd,
Tadworth, Surrey and others at Church House.

Many Methodists, Baptists, United Reformed and Quakers
both locally and at head offices.

Caterers: Valerie, Alan and Pat
Grange Wines, Tadworth, Surrey
Jewellers, photographers, tailors, florists, car hire firms
Alfred Bull & Co. Ltd., Guildford, Surrey (marquees)
W.H. Smith & Son Ltd. (stationers)

INTRODUCTION

The overwhelming majority of the population take the marriage vows at least once during their lifetime.

In anticipation of that romantic event most girls, during their impressionable 'teens, take a few starry-eyed peeps through the pages of women's magazines and read avidly of marriages of well-known stars and public figures.

The men, of course, pretend a lesser romance and express to all who will heed them, almost to the point of no return, their intention of evading the 'walk up the aisle'.

But the result is usually the same; some registrar, somewhere, sometime will link their names in his register with those of their partners. And when that time comes, the man will willingly – or unwillingly – fall into line with his future wife's insistent wishes that the wedding be solemnized with all the ancient tradition and ceremony that she will claim as her right.

Yet, despite the seriousness of the step and the 'so long as you both shall live' finality of their vows, few engaged couples give much thought to the legal obligations involved.

This book is therefore designed to satisfy the bride's eager wish to know and so be able to follow the exact details of the formalities and the long-established customs expected of a wedding – and at least to give the bridegroom some little insight into the legal requirements that must be met before a marriage can take place.

With the passing of the years, though the laws concerning marriage, and the subsequent responsibilities of a man and his wife towards one another, have changed considerably, the etiquette has varied but little. Only in the selection of a marriage partner has the modern girl succeeded in breaking through the strict conventions of her grandmother's day.

In those bygone days a girl would have little say in the so very important matter of choosing her own husband. If she came from a 'good' family she would have been so closely chaperoned that there would have been very few opportunities for her to mix with the younger members of the male sex, and however amenable her parents might have been – or rather, her father might have been – she would have had very little experience on which to make her choice.

And the young man who, though he had had the opportunity of meeting quite a bevy of eligible young ladies, would rarely have been afforded the privilege of a private conversation with any one of them. The result was that when the time came for him to approach a girl's father with a request to be allowed to offer her his 'hand and his heart', his choice of the maiden was likely to have been based on nothing more emotional than her pretty face, her social status and the depth of her father's purse.

And in due course as he knelt before her, she would most probably have received his: 'I have the honour to lay at your feet ...', in fluttering excitement and reply breathlessly: 'I thank you for the honour you have done me and ...', knowing that the young man had been approved by her father – otherwise he would never have been given the opportunity to make his proposal.

And perhaps because she would be kept in ignorance of any alternative suitor, perhaps too because she was rising twenty, her acceptance of the kneeling swain could almost have been taken for granted – happily or otherwise.

Today, the proposal is likely to be made without any reference to either sets of parents and may very well consist of the young man's: 'What about it?', and his beloved's unflurried: 'Why not?' in acceptance.

But the sincerity of both will probably be the deeper because neither will be entering the compact entirely ignorant of the other's character, and neither will have been dragooned into the engagement.

From that moment on the prospective bridegroom will be on 'pins-and-needles' until the whole business is over and done with. He will be glad to know, and very ready to point out to his bride-to-be, that the legal requirements for a marriage are simple so long as each is free to marry the other and that they are both over 18 or have their parents' consent.

All that is necessary is for the banns or intention to marry to be published and then, in due time, for them to spend less than ten minutes in front of a Registrar and two witnesses, and to sign the register thereafter.

But almost always he will find it useless to point out to his bride that all the ancient trappings, religious services and public receptions in the world, will do nothing towards making the marriage more binding either in law or in social acceptance. She will most surely expect to be allowed to pass from her parents care to that of her husband with all due ceremony; she will wish to meet all her friends on that day of days, to receive their good wishes – a bride is never 'congratulated' – and she will not easily be persuaded to surrender her undoubted right to queen it for a day.

But to whom can she turn for details of the ceremonial, of the prescribed protocol and of the established order of events of the great occasion? Her parents would seem to be the obvious source of information, of course, but their memories of their own wedding will be twenty or more years dim.

Their friends? Are they absolutely sure?

Why not within these pages?

1

CAN YOU MARRY
A RELATION?
THE LEGAL POINTS

Certain marriages are prohibited where the couple are held to be too closely related. The Book of Common Prayer lists the forbidden marriages as follows:

A man may not marry his
mother, daughter, father's mother, mother's mother, son's daughter, daughter's daughter, sister, father's daughter, mother's daughter, wife's mother, wife's daughter, father's wife, son's wife, father's father's wife, mother's father's wife, wife's father's mother, wife's mother's mother, wife's son's daughter, wife's daughter's daughter, son's son's wife, daughter's son's wife, father's sister, mother's sister, brother's daughter or sister's daughter.

A woman may not marry her
father, son, father's father, mother's father, son's son, brother, father's son, mother's son, husband's father, husband's son, mother's husband, daughter's husband, father's mother's husband, mother's mother's husband, husband's father's father, husband's mother's father, husband's son's son, husband's daughter's son, son's daughter's husband, daughter's daughter's husband, father's brother, mother's brother, brother's son or sister's son.

The terms 'brother' and 'sister' include half-blood relationships.

The Marriage (Enabling) Act (England, Scotland & Wales) and the Matrimonial Causes (Northern Ireland) Order 1978 followed on from earlier Acts and permit a man's marriage to his deceased wife's sister, aunt or niece, deceased brother's or uncle's or nephew's widow, deceased wife's brother's daughter, deceased wife's sister's daughter, father's deceased brother's widow, mother's deceased brother's widow, deceased wife's father's sister, deceased wife's mother's sister, brother's deceased son's widow and sister's deceased son's widow.

The Marriage (Prohibited Degree of Relationship) Act 1986 (for England, Scotland and Wales, but not Northern Ireland) allows a man to marry his mother-in-law, step-daughter, step-mother, or daughter-in-law without having to obtain a private Act of Parliament. The Act also allows a woman to marry her father-in-law, step-son, step-father, or son-in-law. However, there are certain other conditions which have to be met before the marriages can take place; in particular, for marriages between in-laws, the former spouses will have to have died. Marriages under this Act can take place by Licence or by a Superintendent Registrar's certificate, but not in church after the publication of banns.

A clergyman has the right to refuse to solemnize any marriage where the degree of relationship between the couple is forbidden by the church, but if he so wishes he may allow another clergyman to use his church for the purpose.

A Superintendent Registrar, however, must marry a couple so long as they are legally entitled to marry.

If either party has been married previously, he or she must produce to the Superintendent Registrar documentary proof of their legal ability to re-marry. Where the original partner has died a death certificate is necessary to establish that proof, and where he or she has been divorced, the decree absolute is required. A decree *nisi* is not enough in England and Wales. In Scotland a divorce becomes absolute as soon as it is granted.

In England and Wales both parties to a marriage must have reached the age of 18, unless they have the consent of their parents, or guardians. Such permission must be given in writing and signed by both the minor's parents or guardians.

Where the parents or guardians are abroad their signature to the letter of consent needs to be properly witnessed, usually by a notary public or perhaps a consul.

Where there is neither a parent nor a guardian, a minor has the right to apply to the courts for permission to marry and similarly, where he or she feels that a parent's or guardian's permission is being unreasonably refused, an application to overrule their decision can be made to the same court.

In Scotland, any two persons, regardless of where they live, may marry provided that they are both 16 years of age on the day of their marriage, that they are unmarried, that they are not related to one another, that they are not of the same sex, that they are capable of understanding the nature of a marriage ceremony and of consenting to marriage, and that the marriage would be regarded as valid in any foreign country to which either party belongs.

In all cases there must be at least two witnesses to the marriage – excluding the clergyman and the Registrar – who must be over 18 years old.

2

MODERN ENGAGEMENT DETAILS

An engagement is a much less formal affair than it was in the years gone by. It is still a contract, of course, though not in itself unbreakable without recourse to law.

However, losses caused to either party, through the other calling off the engagement, may well become the subject of a legal wrangle. This usually takes the form of a claim by the disappointed girl against the man who has broken off their engagement, for the cost of, perhaps, the linen, the bedding and other household items she has bought from her own savings towards their joint home. She may add to that any debts she has incurred towards the wedding arrangements, such as the reception, that cannot readily be cancelled – and for any other expenses she has contracted in consequence of the promise of marriage.

If, on the other hand, it is the girl who has put an end to the engagement, the man may feel justified in claiming the return of the engagement ring he has bought her, and for the return of any other valuable pieces of jewellery that he may have presented to her on the understanding that she was to become his wife.

The claims of either party would only have substance, however, if it could be proved that they were incurred only because of the wedding and represented nothing more than a financial loss because of the declared intention of one or other of them not to proceed with the marriage.

Damages for breach of promise are unlikely to succeed today and consequently the project of being able to heal a broken heart with a nice fat cheque is too remote to be worth more than a moment's thought — and surely, a broken engagement is far, far better than to become the unwanted partner in an unhappy marriage?

Usually, an engagement is accepted nowadays as a public expression of the intention of a man and a girl to marry. The announcement is necessary to justify their absence from many of the gatherings of their friends, and to establish their wish to be invited to parties as a couple — to make it clear that neither of them remains free to listen to further proposals of marriage.

Parents are not heeded so carefully, or always informed, before the modern girl and her man decide to announce their engagement. Much of this attitude is due to the high earning capacity of today's young man — and indeed, that of his fiancée — and they are therefore less dependent on their parents.

However, parents are still entitled to some courtesy and as the odds are that they will in any event pay for the wedding and the reception — if nothing more — it is perhaps wise not to jeopardise their goodwill through negligence and bad manners.

Correctly, the bride's parents should be the first to be told of the decision. To ask their 'consent' is no longer general — unless, of course, the girl is under age. Then follows the man's parents — and thereafter the announcement may be broadcast as widely as the couple should desire.

The formality of an announcement in the press is much more rare than it used to be; most people are told as and when the couple happen to meet them. But if the announcement is made through the newspapers, it is proper to inform relatives and close friends verbally in advance. See Chapter 10 for wording of announcement, invitations, etc.

The next consideration is the engagement ring. It is thought to set the seal on the betrothal of the pair and is in itself a warning to other young men not to poach.

However, though an engagement ring is still the prized possession of most girls who have 'found their man' – and remains the prized token of those who have subsequently married – its intrinsic value is perhaps less of an assurance of the young man's depth of feeling today, than of the common sense of the pair who have taken into careful consideration their financial station, prospects and intentions.

Many engaged couples give a lot of thought to the amount that should be spent from their resources on such practical things as a down-payment on a house, the quantity and quality of furniture they can afford to purchase, before entering too deeply into hire purchase commitments and even whether or not they should own a car – before estimating what will be left with which to buy the symbol of their engagement.

But however intrinsically valueless the ring, its symbolic superstition makes it almost a 'must'.

Instead of the more usual diamonds, it is common for a couple to set aside only a limited sum for the ring and economise by selecting a cheaper stone. Cubic zirconia or man-made diamonds are increasingly popular, and birthstones come and go in popularity with current fashion.

Birthstones are generally accepted as being for the

January girl	**Garnets,** meaning	Constancy
February	**Amethysts**	Sincerity
March	**Bloodstones**	Courage
April	**Diamonds**	Purity
May	**Emeralds**	Hope
June	**Pearls** or **Agates**	Health
July	**Rubies**	Passion
August	**Sardonyx**	Married happiness
September	**Sapphires**	Repentance
October	**Topaz**	A lovable nature
November	**Opals**	Cheerfulness
December	**Turquoise** or **Lapis Lazuli**	Unselfishness

The majority of wedding rings sold are nine carat gold, and, when buying the engagement ring, it is just as well to consider this as most brides like their rings to be the same colour! The nine carat rings will stand up to the friction of two rubbing together better than a higher carat. There is also a choice of white gold or platinum. In the past a plain gold band was most common but now there is a wide range of patterned rings to choose from.

In return for the engagement ring, it is usual for the girl to give her betrothed an engagement present – again, of course, limited in value to the means at her disposal after more practical matters have been considered. A gold chain or tie clip or some piece of jewellery such as a signet ring are the more usual gifts for such an occasion.

Though the engaged couple are expected from now on to be kept very busy with the arrangements for their future; the wedding itself, the reception afterwards, the honeymoon, their new home and the furniture that is needed for it – even the trivialities of negotiations with the Electricity Board, the Gas Board and so on and so on, they still have to give some thought to their social obligations.

The engagement party is the most urgent of these and it usually takes place on the day the announcement is made in the press or shortly afterwards. It is at that party that the official announcement of the engagement is made – if it has not already been published in the press.

It is obvious that the engagement party should be held at a very early date after the decision of the couple to marry. It would be difficult to maintain the secret for long in any event and the party loses a lot of its glamour if it is staged long after everybody knows the reason for it and all the congratulations and good wishes have been expressed.

Long engagements are often considered unnecessary and a little undignified, but if the wedding is to be conducted with all the trappings, on a day and time convenient to most of the guests, and a reception to follow, a certain lapse of time is necessary. Many couples are anxious to marry; all of them to prefer much the same date and reception rooms, the same honeymoon hotels and even the same photographer – which means that a good deal of planning is necessary before arrangements can be finalised.

The engagement party is usually a most informal affair and leaves the couple with a wide choice at their disposal. Again the first consideration must be the cost, though it is quite usual for the bride's parents to pay for it, whatever the scale. But as the same people are generally expected to have to pay for the wedding reception in due course, it can be quite a strain on them if thought isn't given to the matter from the very beginning.

The party may be held at either of the parents' homes, though again it is more usual to hold it at the bride's home. It is her father who makes the official announcement of the engagement.

It might be confined to a family party of, say, both sets of parents, brothers and sisters – and maybe those grandparents who are able to be there. The numbers can be increased, of course, though a lot of care must be exercised in the selection. Aunts are inclined to be upset if they have been left out for a close friend and close friends are likely to be resentful if some long neglected relative is included instead of them. Tact is essential.

Of course the numbers can be expanded ad infinitum by taking a hall for the occasion, but it is better to make the occasion as intimate as possible. If larger numbers are to be invited than it is possible to cater for at home, a restaurant is the better place for the party. Everything is supplied, cooked and served – and even the bride's mother has a chance to enjoy herself.

However, even here the guests should be selected with care. It is quite usual for the young couple and their equally young friends to go on from the dinner party in the restaurant – or even from their home – to perhaps a disco dance or a night club afterwards. And the older generation will not be expected to accompany them. Nor should the parents resent being abandoned by the younger element.

The arrangements for the party in a restaurant or a hotel

are quite straightforward. The hotelier or the *restaurateur* will advise you of exactly what you should do to make the occasion a success. He will advise on the menu, the table decorations, the seating, the wines and even on the speeches if the host is at all doubtful about the procedure.

The meal itself need not be too costly, depending of course on the menu, the standard of the hotel or restaurant and the style of the service. Wines will add considerably to the bill if a lot of discretion is not used. Nor is it necessary to have wines. Perhaps a sherry or port with the speeches – and always of course fruit juice or other soft drinks.

For those who might like to spread their wings on the party there are a few suggestions for menus in a subsequent chapter and also what wines could be served with them both economically and as a 'grand gesture'.

The young couple will of course be given the place of honour at the table and if the party is given at home, they will be excused from the usual chores of serving and washing-up afterwards. The bride's parents will sit next to her while the bridegroom's will find their places at his side. This of course will be varied at the wedding reception after they are married. The bride will sit on her groom's left side as always.

The only speeches that are required are two. The first will be made by the bride's father when he either announces the engagement of his daughter or wishes them both health and happiness. The bridegroom replies on behalf of himself and his bride in proposing the health of their parents.

The speeches are usually light-hearted as it is a happy occasion and other toasts may be drunk if the mood of the party permits.

If the younger people are to go on elsewhere or are to dance at the hotel where the engagement party has been given, a move should be made immediately after the speeches. Either by the couple who will lead their friends away or by the parents who will leave their children to their own devices – depending on whether the further entertainment is to be held there or elsewhere.

As the party is informal, dress is usually lounge suits for

the men and semi-evening wear for the women. Printed invitations are unusual, unless the party is to be wide in scope, and even hand-written invitations are the exception, the telephone being the usual thing.

Place-cards and a table plan are considered unnecessary too. Everybody knows that the engaged couple will occupy the seats of honour and that their parents will sit on either side of them. After that, the bride's father, as the host, will suggest where his guests should sit as they come to the table.

Of course a wise host will know his guests in advance – or find out about those he does not know. This enables him to know who should sit next to whom; it could be pretty disastrous to sit old enemies next to one another! But he still must pay regard to the custom that the sexes should alternate.

Sometimes it happens that the girl and her betrothed come from far apart; maybe the man is a Londoner and his wife to be an Edinburgh girl. Obviously it is impossible to bring everybody who has to be at the party all the way from London, but as the bride's parents are the hosts, the venue will almost certainly be in Scotland. In such an event the girl should try and make it possible to attend a similar party in London. This party will be entirely informal, usually at the man's home or that of his parents and limited to those who were unable to travel north for the official party.

If this is not practicable, the couple should try to bring the two sets of parents together – wherever it can be arranged. And at that gathering there will be no need to invite anyone else – with the possible exception of brothers and sisters and grandparents.

3

PRELIMINARY REQUIREMENTS

Accepting that the couple fulfil the legal qualifications set out in Chapter 1, they must then decide on the form their marriage is to take.

Basically, they have the choice of being married:

1. in accordance with the rites of the Church of England;
2. in accordance with the rites of any other religious denomination;
3. before a Superintendent Registrar in accordance with the Civil Law and without any religious service

Church of England. Those who wish to be married according to the rites of this church will find that only one partner need be baptised if the clergyman is satisfied that a church wedding is appropriate. The Church of England recognises all baptism by the pouring (not sprinkling) of, or immersion in, water provided it is in the name of the Holy Trinity. Baptism for the sole purpose of matrimony is not encouraged, and it is recommended that adult baptism should not take place without the expectation of confirmation.

The venue of the marriage must be in the parish where the couple reside, or if they belong to different parishes, in the parish church of either one of them.

Custom decrees that weddings are solemnized in the

parish church of the bride, though this is a matter of tradition and not of law. It is a convenient custom too, as apart from the symbolism of the man coming to collect his bride, it gives her a chance to say farewell to her friends if she is going elsewhere to live, and it makes the question of arrangements for the reception afterwards a simpler matter for the bride's parents.

It might happen, however, that one or the other of the couple have been in the habit of worshipping in a church outside the parish in which he or she lives. In such a case the wedding may be conducted in that church so long as the party concerned worships there regularly for not less than six months. This would entitle the party concerned to sign the electoral roll of the parish, giving them the right of membership – including the right to be married there. If there are other reasons for wishing to marry in another church, a Special Licence is needed.

There are four ways in which a marriage can be authorised to take place in a church of the Church of England:

(a) by Banns;
(b) by Common Licence;
(c) by Special Licence;
(d) by a certificate issued by a Superintendent Registrar.

(a) The most usual procedure is by the reading of the banns on three successive Sundays in the parish church of each of the engaged couple, and in the parish where one of them is on the electoral roll, if this is the situation.

Naturally, an application must be made to the incumbent of the church in which the couple desire to be married. Only one of them need make the application. If the clergyman is satisfied that the couple are legally qualified to marry, he will arrange to give notice of their intention to the members of his congregation at one of the services on each of the Sundays concerned, permitting anyone who may have reason to doubt their qualifications to make an objection.

The banns must, of course, be read in the parish church of

both the man and the girl, if they reside in different parishes – and they must continue to reside in their particular parishes for the whole of the three weeks during which the banns are read. They must *in addition* be read in the parish church where one or other of them is on the electoral roll if the marriage is to take place there.

The clergyman due to perform the ceremony will require a certificate from the clergyman of the church or churches not being the actual venue of the wedding, but being the parish church of either of the couple, certifying that the banns have in fact been published there too, and that no valid objection has been received.

After the banns have been read for the three specified Sundays without any substantial objection being voiced, the marriage can be solemnized at any time between 8 a.m and 6 p.m. on almost any day thereafter, though the church discourages weddings during Lent. However, there is a time limit of three calendar months to the effectiveness of this authority – and the banns must again be called if the wedding is still intended to take place.

(b) Marriage by Common Licence is usually where the three weeks' delay taken up in the reading of the banns is, for some reason or another, not tolerable or where one or other party is not a British subject, or not an English or Welsh resident. The reason for haste may be legion; a hurried move abroad by the bridegroom to take up a particular post perhaps; or maybe because of a family illness or, too often, because a birth is imminent. Whatever the reason, there is no need for delay nor to declare the reason for the short notice.

Nor are residential qualifications so strict. Only one of the couple need live in the parish where the marriage is to be conducted, and he or she need only have resided in the district for fifteen days, immediately prior to the application. The other party to the marriage is not called upon to produce any residential qualifications.

Only a clear day's notice need be given before the ceremony, thereafter the actual date and time is a matter of arrangement between the couple and the clergyman – with a time limit of three calendar months to the effectiveness of the authority. A new application would have to be made if the marriage had not taken place within that time and it was still intended to go ahead with the ceremony.

The application for such a licence may be made to the incumbent of the church where it is desired to hold the wedding. If he is not able to grant the licence himself, he will be able to advise the couple of the address of the nearest Surrogate or the Diocesan Register for granting Marriage Licences in the Diocese.

The application must be made in person though only one of the parties to the wedding need do so, there is no need for both to go.

(c) Marriage by Special Licence is most unusual and such a licence is only issued on the authority of the Archbishop of Canterbury through the Faculty Office, 1, The Sanctuary, Westminster, London, SW1.

Such a licence would only be granted in the case of emergency and where an ordinary licence would not suffice. The usual reason for the issue of such a licence is because neither of the couple have residential qualifications, or more often, because there is some urgent reason why the ceremony needs to be held outside a church licensed for marriages, or a Register Office or other authorised place; perhaps by a bedside in a hospital or a home where there is a serious illness – to the point of death.

Strangely, neither St. Paul's Cathedral, Westminster Abbey nor the chapel of Buckingham Palace is registered for marriages and weddings conducted therein, even of Royalty, require the Archbishop of Canterbury's Special Licence.

(d) It is possible to obtain a certificate of authorisation for a marriage to be conducted in a church of the Church of England from a Superintendent Registrar but this would not be binding on the incumbent who might well insist on a Common Licence being procured.

In any event it would seem wise to consult the clergyman of the church first – since he may find it difficult because of prior commitments to find a suitable time for the ceremony.

However, if the clergyman is willing to accept such a certificate, no further legal authorisation would be needed.

Such an application needs to be made to the Superintendent Registrar not less than 21 days before the wedding is expected to take place and each of the parties to it must have been resident for not less than seven days in their own district immediately before the notice is entered by the Registrar.

Once the certificate has been issued it is valid for three calendar months; if the wedding is to take place after that time, a new application to the Registrar must be made.

The cost of a Superintendent Registrar's certificate is dependent on whether the couple reside in the same district or in different ones. A full list of all the various fees that relate to the different ways of being married is given in the Appendix on page 147.

It is becoming more and more common to find short preparation courses for those about to marry, run by clergy, the Relate Marriage Guidance Council, and other bodies. If you are offered one of these it may help you to sort out your idea of what the marriage ceremony is *really* about.

The Roman Catholic Church. Where both the man and the girl are Roman Catholics a certificate must be obtained from the Superintendent Registrar of Marriages of the district in which they live, which will also be the district in which they marry. Only one of the parties need attend personally on the Registrar to make the application, but he or she must give all the essential details concerning both. ages, residential qualifications, addresses   and where necessary proof of either divorce or the death of a previous partner.

Civil divorce is not recognised by the Roman Catholic Church. Only in the rarest of circumstances will a re-marriage be countenanced, e.g. if the first marriage was not recognised by the Catholic Church. This would be the case if the first marriage took place in a Register Office, and one of the parties was a Catholic, or if the first marriage had been declared null and void by a Roman Catholic Marriage Tribunal. In either of these cases there will be no bar to the projected wedding so long as the civil law has been met.

If the engaged couple live in different districts, notice must be given to the Superintendent Registrar in both, and to establish their residential qualifications, they must each have resided in the district where his or her application is to be made for at least seven days prior to the notice being entered by the Registrar.

Twenty-one days thereafter the Superintendent Registrar will issue the required certificates – providing that neither notices have resulted in valid objections being raised.

Where it is desired to hold the wedding ceremony within the prescribed twenty-one days after the entry of the notice, the Superintendent Registrar may issue a Superintendent's Licence together with his certificate. This entitles the couple to marry at any time after the elapse of one clear working day after the notice has been given.

Where a Superintendent's Licence is sought, only one of the engaged couple need have residential qualifications, but it consists of the need for that person to have lived for not less than fifteen days continuously in the district where the application is made, immediately prior to the notice being given to the Registrar.

It is well to consult the parish priest concerning the detailed arrangements for the wedding as, though the Registrar's certificate authorises the marriage under the civil law, it does not insist that the church shall carry out the ceremony.

The Roman Catholic Church still requires that the banns be read in the parish church of each of the betrothed – except in the event of one of them not being a Catholic. In such case, no banns are read.

There are differing types of service to solemnize

matrimony too, dependent upon whether one or other of the parties is a non-Catholic.

Generally speaking, a Catholic priest will require up to six months' notice of a projected wedding, and longer if possible. This will enable him to provide for adequate preparation for the couple. Nowadays in most Catholic churches this is regarded as essential, and not only where one of the parties is a non-Catholic.

The Catholic Marriage Advisory Council conduct 'Preparation for Marriage' courses throughout the country and details can be obtained from The Catholic Marriage Advisory Council Headquarters, Clitherow House, 1 Blythe Mews, Blythe Road, London, W14 0NW.

Adequate notice is also required by the ministers of the various *Free Churches* such as the Methodists, Baptists, and United Reformed Church (which includes most Presbyterian and Congregational churches) of marriages intended to be celebrated in their churches.

To comply with the civil law all marriages must take place within a church or a building registered by the Registrar General for the purpose of conducting marriage services. Such marriages must be witnessed by at least two people who have reached the age of 18 and by an 'authorised person'.

The 'authorised person' will be the Registrar, his deputy or more usually a minister of the church who has been authorised by the Registrar General.

Many of the Free churches and Roman Catholic churches are registered under the Marriage Acts but some are not; most of the clergymen of these churches are 'authorised', but by no means all of them.

It is obviously necessary to check on these points, so that if necessary the couple when applying to the Superintendent Registrar for a certificate, can arrange for a civil ceremony to take place in the Register Office. Where the church is not registered for the conduct of marriages, they should inform the Superintendent Registrar of the need for a Registrar's presence at the church, where it is registered, but where the minister performing the ceremony is not an 'authorised person'.

The fact that a minister is not an authorised person does not preclude him from conducting the marriage service, but it does require the attendance of the Registrar or his deputy.

The details of the conditions attached to the issue of a Superintendent Registrar's certificate and licence have been described elsewhere in this chapter and need not be repeated.

The civil law is varied in the case of a *Jewish Wedding* to permit the ceremony to take place anywhere; in a Synagogue, a private house, a hired hall, or any chosen place, whether registered for the purpose or not. There are no times specified during which the service may be held – though it is usual for the ceremony to be performed in a Synagogue at any convenient time, excluding the hours between sunset on Friday and sunset the following day, Saturday, the Jewish Sabbath. Marriages do not take place, though, on any festival or intermediate days of any festival; on any Fast day; in the three weeks from the Fast of Tammuz to the Fast of Av; and certain weeks during the counting of the Omer. It is unusual for marriages to take place on the eves of Sabbaths or Festivals. For full details, consult your Rabbi or Secretary of the Synagogue.

A Quaker Wedding (Religious Society of Friends), requires, of course, the same recourse to a Superintendent Registrar for a certificate or licence as in all cases, save those of the Church of England. It requires, too, the completion of the Society's own marriage forms.

Marriage according to Quaker usage is subject to approval by their Registering Officers acting for the meeting concerned. Each area monthly meetings (usually comprising a number of local meetings for worship) appoints a Registering Officer: he will give advice and information, and is responsible for issuing the forms and registering the marriage.

A non-member of the Society will need to have the written

support of two adult members who are satisfied that he/she is in agreement with the Quaker view of marriage.

Notice of the intended marriage is given at the close of the Sunday morning meetings where each of the parties are members or where they usually worship, or in the district where they live.

If no written notice of objections is received, the Registering Officer completes a form to this effect and arrangements for the wedding can then proceed.

Civil Ceremony. There is no need for a marriage to be solemnized either in a place of worship or by a minister of religion. Only the civil law need be heeded and such a marriage in a Register Office, conducted by a Superintendent Registrar is as completely binding in law as any conducted under the auspices of any religious body.

There are many reasons why a couple may elect to be married in a Register Office under civil law alone; they may subscribe to no religious beliefs, they may be of different persuasions and prefer to marry under a neutral authority, they may be debarred by the church because one or both have been divorced.

Absolute secrecy is not, of course, possible as the intention to marry is published by an entry in the Superintendent Registrar's 'notice book' which is available for all to inspect. Also, all notices are exhibited on the Superintendent Registrar's notice board. However, such an inspection is rarely made by unsuspecting parties, and it is unusual, except where the couple are personalities who attract the attention of the press, for the intention to leak out in advance.

For such a marriage, notice must be given to the Superintendent Registrar in the district where the couple live and where they intend to marry. Such notice must be given in person and a detailed application form must be completed.

The person giving notice must state the names, ages, addresses, marital status, occupation, and where the marriage is to take place, with the period each has resided there, and a declaration must be made stating that there is no lawful impediment to the marriage.

If either of the parties is under 18 years of age, and marrying for the first time, the consent in writing of both parents or other legal guardians is required.

Both parties to the marriage must have lived in the district where they wish to marry for at least seven days immediately preceding the giving of notice to the Superintendent Registrar. If they come from different districts, separate applications must be made in each district.

If either of the parties has been married previously, he or she will have to produce proof to the Superintendent Registrar, either in the form of a death certificate or a decree absolute, that there is no legal barrier to a second marriage.

If no objection is received and verified within twenty-one days of the entry of notice, the Superintendent Registrar will issue his certificate and the marriage can be conducted as soon thereafter as is convenient.

If, for some reason or other, the couple wish to be married within the prescribed twenty-one days, they may apply to the Superintendent Registrar for marriage by Certificate and Licence. The conditions for its issue are similar to those required for the certificate, except that only one of the parties need give notice and that one of the parties has been resident in the district for not less than fifteen days immediately preceding the giving of notice.

If there is no objection, the licence and the certificate will be issued after the expiry of one clear working day, other than a Sunday, Christmas Day, or Good Friday, from the entry of the notice, and the marriage can take place in the Register Office at any time thereafter (within three months).

Serving members of the *Royal Navy* who are sea-going are not penalized by their inability to establish residential qualifications ashore. In any such case the sailor may make application to his Captain to have the banns read aboard his ship during morning service on three successive Sundays; the banns also being read in the bride's church, where the ceremony will eventually take place, at the same time.

At the end of the qualifying period of twenty-one days, the Captain will make an entry in his Banns of Marriage register and issue a certificate stating that the banns have been called and that no valid objections to the marriage have been brought to his attention. This certificate must then be passed to the clergyman ashore who is to perform the wedding ceremony.

When it is intended that the marriage should take place before a Superintendent Registrar in a Register Office, or before a clergyman of a church other than that of the Church of England, the seaman should complete a form of notice in the presence of his Captain and that officer should countersign it as a witness.

After twenty-one days, the Captain will issue a certificate informing the Superintendent Registrar that due notice was given him by the seaman, and that no valid objection had been brought to his notice.

As soon as the bridegroom's certificate has been issued, the bride must give similar notice to the Superintendent Registrar in the district where she lives and where the marriage is to be conducted, and to the officiating clergyman if a church service is intended.

Please see Appendix, page 148, for civil fees.

4

NORTHERN IRELAND AND SCOTLAND

Marriage regulations and laws are different in Northern Ireland and Scotland.

Church of Ireland. A marriage may be authorised to take place in a church of the Church of Ireland in four different ways:

(a) by Banns;
(b) by Licence;
(c) by Special Licence;
(d) by a certificate issued by a Registrar.

(a) Where both parties to the marriage are Protestant Episcopalians, the banns may be read in the church where the ceremony is to take place, subject to the rites of the church. The clergyman who is expected to conduct the service must be consulted about the arrangements.

(b) To obtain a licence one or both of the parties to the marriage must be Protestant Episcopalian. The licence is obtainable from a Church of Ireland Licenser for a marriage in a church within his district. One of the parties must have resided for at least seven days in the Licenser's district immediately prior to service of notice of the proposed marriage. The Licenser will send copies of the notice to the clergymen of the places of worship which the parties attend.

Seven days after notice has been served on him, the Licenser may issue his licence. Immediately before the grant of the licence, one of the parties must make an oath or declaration which includes a clause to the effect that one of them has had his or her usual residence for fourteen days immediately preceding within the district attached to the church in which the marriage is to be solemnized.

The marriage must take place within three months from the date of notice.

The address of the District Church of Ireland Licenser can be obtained from the clergyman at the church where the ceremony is to take place.

(c) A Special Licence may be granted by a Bishop of the Church of Ireland, provided one or both of the parties to the marriage are Protestant Episcopalians. This authorises the marriage to take place at any time and in any place authorised by the Bishop and within his jurisdiction.

(d) A Registrar's Certificate may be obtained, where one or both of the parties are Protestant Episcopalians, authorising the marriage to take place in a church. The application for the certificate must be made to the Registrar in the district where the couple live. If they live in different districts, the Registrar in each of them must provide a certificate. The Registrar must send a copy of the notice of marriage to the clergymen of the places of worship attended by the parties and if different to either of these, to the clergymen of the church where the marriage is to be solemnized.

At least one of the parties must have resided in the district attached to the church where the marriage is to be celebrated, for not less than fourteen days immediately preceding the declaration of the fact.

Presbyterian Churches. Though the form and discipline of the Presbyterian Church in Ireland, the Non-Subscribing Presbyterian Church of Ireland and the Reformed Presbyterian Church of Ireland differ somewhat, the authorisation for the celebration of marriage is similar. In the case of the Evangelical Presbyterian Church and the Free Presbyterian Church the procedure is as with 'Other Religious Bodies' set out later.

Authorisation may be obtained by:

(a) **Licence**
(b) **Special Licence**
(c) **Banns**

(a) To obtain a licence, which is the normal procedure, one or both of the parties must be of the particular Presbyterian Church involved. If one or both should be under 18 years of age (21 in the Republic of Ireland) a special Consent Form must be obtained and signed by the parents or guardians.

Application must first be made to the minister of the congregation of which one of them has been a member for at least the past month. He will then issue a certificate to that effect, which should be produced to one of the Licensing Ministers, appointed by the district Presbytery, at least seven days before he is expected to grant the licence. The licence must be produced to the officiating minister before the marriage service takes place.

Before the grant of the licence, he or she, whoever has obtained the certificate from the minister, must make a Declaration (or Oath) which includes a statement to the effect that one of the parties has resided for fifteen days, immediately preceding, within the Presbytery area. (Regular connection with a congregation of the Presbytery may sometimes be taken as a 'residential' qualification.)

The marriage must take place within three calendar months from the date of entry of notice in the Licensing Minister's Notice Book, and it must also take place within one calendar month from the date of the licence.

(b) A Special Licence may be obtained authorising the marriage to take place at any time or place in Ireland. The issuing authority is the Moderator of the General Assembly of the Presbyterian Church in Ireland or the Moderator of Synod for the other two Presbyterian churches.

One or both of the parties must be a member of a congregation of the Church body presided over by the Moderator granting the Special Licence.

A Declaration (or Oath) including a statement to this effect must be signed before a Justice of the Peace.

There are no special requirements in respect of residence in advance notice, but Consent forms must be completed in respect of any party under age. A Special Licence is valid for three months.

(c) Where both parties to the marriage are members of the same Presbyterian body, banns may be published in the church or churches of which the parties are members. The ministers concerned will each require six days' notice of the intention, after which they will read the banns to their congregations on the following successive three Sundays.

The wedding must take place in one of the churches where the banns have been published.

It is not legal to publish banns where one of the parties is a member of another Church body or the wedding is to take place in the church of another body.

It must be emphasised, as indicated above, that for banns both parties must be members of the same Presbyterian denomination, not just both Presbyterians but of different Church bodies, even when these are in full mutual relationship, such as applies between the Presbyterian Church in Ireland and the Church of Scotland. This must be emphasised because almost all the requests that come to the ministers for the calling of banns come from other denominations, in Ireland or Britain, where this is the normal procedure.

The marriage legislation basically applies to both Northern Ireland and the Irish Republic, except that in the Republic consent from parent or guardian must be obtained for those under 21, and not 18 years of age as in Northern Ireland.

The Roman Catholic Church. Marriages according to the rites and ceremonies of the Roman Catholic Church may be solemnized:

(a) by Episcopal Licence;
(b) after publication of Banns;
(c) by Licence;
(d) by a certificate issued by a Registrar of Marriages.

(a) and (b): Both parties must be Roman Catholic. The proceedings are regulated by the law of the Roman Catholic Church and the parties should apply to their parish priest or priests for information about the steps to be taken.

(c) One or both of the parties must be Roman Catholic. A licence may be obtained from a person nominated to issue licences by a Bishop of the Roman Catholic Church. Where only one of the parties is a Roman Catholic, notice in writing must be given to the person empowered to issue licences seven days before the licence shall be issued and that person must send copies of the notice to the clergymen of the places of worship which the parties attend.

(d) When one of the parties is other than a Roman Catholic, a Registrar's Certificate may be obtained authorising the marriage to take place in a Roman Catholic church.

Other Religious Bodies. Three forms of authorisation for a marriage are available to the members of other churches:

(a) by Registrar's Certificate;
(b) by Registrar's Licence;
(c) by Special Licence (in certain cases)

(a) A Registrar's Certificate for marriage in a church or registered building in his district is obtainable twenty-one clear days after notice of marriage has been served. Residence within the Registrar's district is necessary. If both parties reside in the district, a residence of not less than seven days immediately prior to the service of notice is necessary in respect of both, or if one of the parties resides in another district a residence of at least seven days must have been fulfilled there, and notice also given to the Registrar of that district, and his certificate obtained. The Registrar(s) must send copies of the notice(s) to the ministers of the places of worship which the parties attend and, if different to either of these, to the clergyman of the church or building where the marriage is to be solemnized.

(b) If the wedding is to be held at shorter notice than that applicable under a Registrar's Certificate, a licence may be obtained from the District Registrar in whose district the church or building is situated. This permits the solemn-ization of the marriage seven clear days after the date of notice.

If both parties reside in the district, one must have resided there for not less than fifteen days and the other for not less than seven days immediately preceding the service of notice. If one of the parties resides in another district a residence of fifteen days must have been fulfilled there and notice also given to the Registrar of that district and the Registrar of the district in which the marriage is to take place will require the certificate of the Registrar of the other district before he will issue his licence. Copies of the notice(s) will be issued as outlined under **(a)**.

Under **(a)** and **(b)**, a marriage must take place within three months from the date of notice.

(c) A Special Licence may be obtained authorising the marriage to take place at any time and at any place in Ireland if one or both parties belong to the Baptist Church, the Congregational Union of Ireland, or the Methodist or Wesleyan Church in Ireland.

Methodists. Members of the Methodist Church in Ireland may be married by a Registrar's Certificate, by a Registrar's Licence or by a Special Licence issued by the Secretary of the Conference of the Methodist Church in Ireland.

Quakers. Members of the Society of Friends may be married either by a Registrar's Certificate or by Special Licence issued by the Clerk to the Yearly Meeting of the Society of Friends in Ireland.

Jews. Marriages between Jews require the authorisation of a Registrar's Certificate, but they need not marry in the district where they live.

Civil Marriages. Where a couple desire to be married without any religious ceremony, they may apply to a Registrar to be married in his Office.

The conditions are similar to those applicable for the issue of either a Registrar's Certificate or Licence (see Other Religious Bodies).

Copies of the notice must be sent to the clergymen of the places of worship usually attended by the parties or if either party has not attended a place of worship during the month preceding the giving of notice, the notice must be advertised, at the expense of the parties, in a local newspaper, once at least, in two consecutive weeks.

Where one of the parties is resident outside Northern Ireland. In the case of a marriage pursuant to the licence of a Church of Ireland or Presbyterian Licenser, if one party resides in Northern Ireland and fulfils the statutory conditions, that party can take all the steps necessary to obtain the licence, and the residence of the other party is immaterial.

For a marriage in a church of the Church of Ireland in Northern Ireland, when both parties are Protestant Episcopalians, and one of them resides in England, it is lawful for banns to be published in respect of the latter party in the parish or place of residence in England, banns being also duly published in the parish or district of the party resident in Northern Ireland.

In the case of an intended marriage in Northern Ireland for which authority from a Registrar is required, and where one of the parties resides in England or Wales, the party so resident should serve notice on, and (seven days afterwards) obtain a certificate from the Superintendent Registrar of the district of residence. Seven days after the issue of such a certificate, its production to the Registrar in Northern Ireland enables him to issue the necessary authority, provided that the party resident in his district has taken the requisite steps there.

Where the marriage is to take place in Great Britain (not Northern Ireland). Where a marriage is to be solemnized in England or Wales by the 'certificate' procedure and one of the parties resides in Northern Ireland, the party resident in Northern Ireland should serve notice on the Registrar of the district where he or she resides and obtain the Registrar's Certificate for production to the Superintendent Registrar of the district in England or Wales where the marriage is to take place. Where the marriage is intended to take place in a church of the Church of England, it is within the power of the incumbent to refuse to act upon such a certificate, and his prior consent should accordingly be obtained. (The party resident in England or Wales must also take the requisite steps there.)

If the marriage is to take place in Scotland, the party resident in Northern Ireland should obtain a *marriage notice* form and explanatory leaflet from the Registrar for the Registration District in Scotland in which the marriage is to be solemnized. The marriage notice must be returned to the Registrar. It is not necessary to take up residence in Scotland.

SCOTLAND

There are several differences between the marriage laws of England and Wales, and Scotland:

(a) Where the banns must be read in a church of the Church of England on three successive Sundays, banns are no longer required for a religious marriage in Scotland.

(b) Residence is not a requirement but both parties to a marriage, whether religious or civil, must give at the very least fifteen days' notice before the date of the proposed marriage.

(c) In Scotland, as in the rest of the United Kingdom, the legal minimum age for marriage is 16, but parental consent is not required by law in Scotland for those under 18 years old.

Each of the parties must complete and submit a marriage notice, which you can obtain from any registrar of births, deaths and marriages in Scotland. You will find the local address in your telephone directory. You will need to take or send the following documents with the appropriate fee to the registrar for the district in which the marriage is to take place: Your birth certificate; a copy of the decree of divorce or annulment if you have been married before and the marriage has been dissolved (a decree nisi is not acceptable);

and if you are a widow or widower, the death certificate of your former spouse.

Timing is most important. The marriage notices must be submitted early enough to enable the registrar to satisfy himself that you are free to marry one another. He should have the notices four weeks before the marriage, but if either party has been married before, the registrar should receive the notices six weeks beforehand.

Every person giving notice has to sign a declaration that the particulars and information they have given on the marriage notice are correct. As a safeguard against bigamous marriages a subsequent check of the information is made centrally.

When he is satisfied there is no legal impediment to the marriage, the registrar will prepare a Marriage Schedule from the information you have given him. This Schedule is most important – no marriage can proceed without it.

If you are having a church wedding the Marriage Schedule will be issued to you by the registrar. It cannot be issued more than seven days before the marriage and you will be told when to call for it. The Schedule cannot be collected for you by a relative or friend, it will only be issued to the prospective bride or bridegroom. The Marriage Schedule *must* be produced before the marriage ceremony to the person performing the marriage.

Immediately after the church service the Marriage Schedule must be signed by the bride and bridegroom, by the person performing the marriage and by two witnesses who are 16 years or over. It must then be returned to the registrar within three days so that he can register the marriage.

If you are having a civil marriage, the Marriage Schedule will not be issued to you but the registrar will have it at the marriage ceremony for signature. Subsequently he can register the marriage. A fee for the civil marriage is payable to the registrar in advance. After the marriage has been registered you can obtain copies of the marriage certificate from the registrar on payment of the appropriate fee.

Marriage in the Church of Scotland. If you wish to be married in the Church of Scotland, go and see the minister before completing the notice of marriage.

Marriage of other Denominations. A religious marriage, whether Christian or non-Christian (Jewish, Moslem, Hindu, etc.) may be solemnized only by a minister, clergyman, pastor, priest or other person entitled to do so under the Marriage (Scotland) Act 1977.

Civil Marriages. The procedures have been detailed in the preceding paragraphs.

If you live in England or Wales and you hope to marry a person living in Scotland, or you both live in England or Wales and your intended has a parent living in Scotland you should give notice of the wedding to the Superintendent Registrar in the district in which you must have lived for the preceding seven days. The person you are marrying should, however, give notice in Scotland as explained earlier. The certificate issued by the Superintendent Registrar in England or Wales should be sent to the registrar in Scotland where the marriage is to be held. This certificate will obviate the need for the partner living in England or Wales to give notice in Scotland.

If you live outside the United Kingdom the normal procedure of giving notice to the registrar in Scotland must be followed. In addition to the documents mentioned earlier you will need a *certificate of no impediment* issued by the competent authority (usually the civil authority) to the effect that you are free to marry. If any document is in a language other than English, you should produce a certified translation. Without this certificate it may not be possible for you to be married in Scotland.

5

MARRIAGE FOR THOSE LIVING ABROAD, FOREIGNERS, ETC.

Marriage regulations and laws are not the same for foreigners marrying in the United Kingdom, nor do they apply in quite the same way to British subjects marrying abroad. Also, where a British subject intends to marry a foreigner – abroad or at home – there is always the matter of the girl's nationality after her marriage.

The engaged couple would be well advised to consult the various authorities. In Britain an interview should be sought with the clergyman or leader of the religious sect involved. If there is to be no religious service, advice will be available at the various Superintendent Registrars' offices, the addresses of which may be found in the local telephone directory.

If a British subject intends to marry abroad, he or she should consult a member of the British Embassy, Legation or Consulate in the country and district where the marriage is to take place, irrespective of whether both parties are British or one of them happens to be a national of the country concerned.

Similarly, a foreigner wishing to marry in the United Kingdom, whether to a British subject or to someone of their own nationality, should consult his or her resident representative in Britain to make sure that their marriage will be accepted as legally binding in their own country.

6

THE MARRIAGE OF DIVORCED PERSONS

Church of England. The Church of England expressly forbids the re-marriage of a divorced person during the lifetime of a previous partner.

A clergyman has the legal right to refuse to marry in church anyone whose previous partner is still alive, irrespective of whether the person concerned is the injured or the guilty party.

Nor can he be compelled to permit such a marriage to take place in his church. Nor can he be compelled to conduct a service for anyone who has re-married under civil law. Not all clergymen refuse however. No Common or Special Licence will be issued for such a marriage.

When the couple, one of whose marriages has previously been dissolved, is anxious to have some form of religious ceremony, most clergymen will be very willing to hold a service of prayer and blessing. Although strictly speaking this service should be both quiet and private, at the discretion of the clergyman and subject to the regulations issued by the General Synod it can be fuller and richer although it must be made quite clear that it is *not*, in fact, a marriage service.

Roman Catholic Church. The Church of Rome does not recognise the right of the civil authorities to dissolve a marriage through divorce. In consequence, normally there can be no 're-marriage' where there is a partner surviving.

There are, however, some circumstances in which the Roman Catholic Church will not recognise the previous marriage. This will be the case when a Catholic was previously married outside the authority of the Catholic church. It will also be verified where the Catholic authorities, in the form of the Marriage Tribunal, has declared a previous marriage to be null and void. In such cases, the Church will be prepared to marry that person – provided of course that he or she has the legal right in civil law; by being divorced by the State from their original partner.

Free Churches. The question of the re-marriage of a divorced person is very much at the discretion of each particular minister. Some of them firmly believe that the original contract is binding for life, others may accept the fact that the wronged party is being unjustly penalized and yet others will consider that everyone is entitled to another chance.

In consequence an approach to a minister is necessary – and some couples have approached more than one minister before contacting one who is willing to marry them.

The Society of Friends. Though Quakers believe in the sanctity and life-long nature of marriage, they are sympathetic to and understanding of those who have been divorced and wish to marry in a Friends' meeting.

Nevertheless, they are not willing to consider the question of re-marriage without all the circumstances being taken into account. The monthly meeting would need to be satisfied that the person seeking their permission was well known to them and associated with the meeting. It is possible that the matter might be investigated by a small group of Friends so that the monthly meeting might be advised by them without the need to air all the circumstances in public.

The monthly meetings are given discretion whether or not to grant permission to those who wish to re-marry in a Friends' meeting.

Civil Re-marriages. The law of England and Wales recognises a divorced person as single so long as they can produce a decree absolute. Having produced that document, a re-marriage in a Register Office is conducted on exactly the same conditions as those applying to a first marriage.

Scottish divorced persons. The only difference between the various regulations and conditions applying for re-marriage between England and Wales and Scotland concerns the method of divorce.

In England and Wales a decree *nisi* pronounces the divorce, but neither party is free to re-marry until a decree absolute has been obtained. This is obtainable on application by the successful petitioner, six weeks after the decree *nisi.*

In Scotland there is no such thing as a preliminary pronouncement. The decree is absolute, or final, from the moment of the divorce, leaving the divorced persons free to take immediate steps towards re-marriage if they should so desire.

7

OTHER ARRANGEMENTS
YOU MUST MAKE

In the previous chapters the couple will have discovered the procedures by which their marriage may be conducted – and have decided on the one most appropriate and suitable to themselves. And, of course, all other arrangements must depend on the time, the date and the venue of the marriage itself.

The date needs a lot of care in the choosing. In the first place it must coincide with available dates and times at the church where the wedding is to take place, and, of course, with the agreement of the clergyman who will conduct the service.

And in some areas it is difficult to book the arrangements because of the demand by other couples. Saturdays, for instance, are generally reserved for weeks and even months ahead – as weekends are usually the most convenient times for the majority of guests.

The bridegroom's normal holidays from work – and those of the bride as often as not – usually need to coincide with the honeymoon. So, the summer months are a busy time for weddings, Easter, Whitsuntide and August Bank Holidays are popular periods too, and cause queues of wedding parties at churches and register offices up and down the land.

In any event there should be as little haste between the decision to marry and the service itself as possible. Other arrangements might prove just as difficult to conclude, unless there is time in hand.

But once the time and the date of the wedding have been fixed, the bride and groom – and, indeed, the bride's parents – can turn their attention to all the other arrangements that are so necessary to make a success of the occasion.

The bridegroom is least concerned in the making of the arrangements, though he can expect to be consulted by the bride on many matters, and to have to discuss with her some of his own plans.

The honeymoon, for instance; though he will be expected to make all the arrangements for it, obviously his bride will want some say in the plans themselves.

Broadly, the bridegroom's tasks cover:

The selection of his best man and ushers.
His 'stag party'.
The purchase of the wedding ring.

The planning and booking of everything in connection with the honeymoon – not forgetting passports, travellers' cheques and inoculations if needed; the car from the reception to the station or airport if they are to leave by train or air.

Attend to buying or hiring his own wedding clothes.

The bride's list is much more complicated, though the responsibility for most of the items will rest on the shoulders of her parents.

She must:

Decide whether to be married in church or a register office and then complete the arrangements for the wedding service. If it is to be a church wedding she will have to organise the Order of Service, the music and the church decorations.

Select her Chief Bridesmaid, the bridesmaids and perhaps pages, and choose their dresses.

Make out a guest list.

Organise the reception, where to hold it, the menu and the wines.

Organise the wedding cake.

Order the flowers, bouquets, buttonholes and corsages.

Order the wedding cars to the church and to the reception afterwards.

Choose the invitations, have them printed and send them out.

Arrange press announcements.

Book the photographer.

Arrange for the display of their wedding presents.

She will also have to buy, hire or make:

Her wedding gown and all that goes with it.

Her trousseau.

Her going away outfit.

And her luggage.

Apart from the need for consultation concerning plans and arrangements, there must be some discussion concerning the payment of the bills in connection with the wedding. Everything from the decorations to the hire of the cars, the wedding breakfast and the wines, the bridesmaids' dresses, the bouquets, the photographs and even the organists' fees must be met either with a cheque or in cash.

It is usual, but by no means obligatory, for the bride's parents to pay for the reception, the cake and everything concerning the celebration after the service, while the groom meets the cost of the wedding itself (clergyman's fees, organist, licence, etc.), the gifts for the bridesmaids and the honeymoon afterwards.

Naturally, the scale of the marriage and its celebration afterwards must be related to the financial status of those concerned – and where the resources of the parents differ considerably, it is usual for the better situated to pay a full measure towards the event.

The cost to the bride's parents can be considerable and the bridegroom's parents should bear in mind that generally their own share is trivial in comparison.

Account must be taken, too, of what funds are to be held back to help the young couple to start their new life together.

Of course, many a bride is insistent that the wedding day is the high spot in her life, never to be repeated, and she expects it to be treated as such – and if there is anything to spare after the celebrations, maybe she wants the honeymoon to be the talking point of her memories for the rest of her life.

Men are more inclined to favour less publicity and pageantry than their brides, but they are often in collusion with them concerning the scope of their honeymoon.

Other couples view the future rather differently. They realise that a large sum spent on a single day's ceremonies and jollifications plus perhaps a similar sum on a fortnight's honeymoon on the Continent, might be put to more practical and permanent use. A larger down-payment on their home perhaps, less furniture on the H.P. for instance, maybe more elaborate decorations and carpeting in their new house, even a little car that might have had to wait for a couple of years, or needed as a background to his career in business.

The guest list for the wedding and the reception afterwards may require careful thought. Of course the matter presents few problems where neither family have many relations or friends who could expect to be invited but in some families, the numbers may well run into hundreds and even then a little forgetfulness may result in offence being taken where it was not intended.

Other couples may find that their families have a very unbalanced list of friends and relations they wish to invite to the wedding, resulting in the need for a lot of tact, commonsense and maybe a certain amount of generosity.

All these problems need to be solved and minds must be made up quickly, if there isn't a great deal of time to spare. Not only will there be a waiting list for available times and dates at the church or the register office, but almost everything else connected with a wedding is in equally urgent demand.

With holidays being booked nearly six months in advance, honeymoon reservations require equally early consideration – and attention. The printing of invitation cards can rarely be promised under a week or two, dressmaking takes a lot of time and patience and even the wedding cake needs care if it is to be as nice as the bride would like it to be.

The photographer will have a long list of appointments, so will the car hire firm, the florist; the caterer is likely to be booked on many dates, the guests may have prior appointments – and even the hairdresser may not be available at the time required, unless she is given adequate notice.

Most of the items listed above are dealt with in subsequent chapters, but it is well that all concerned should realise the amount of organisation that is going to be necessary if the wedding is to be the happy day it should be.

8

THE STAG PARTY

It has long been the custom for the prospective bridegroom to entertain his bachelor friends at a party on the night before his wedding – and as you can imagine, such affairs are generally regarded with a tolerant eye, by the older folk, as being a last wild fling before the responsibilities of matrimony descend on the young man's shoulders.

But too often, the effect on the bridegroom and the best man has been carried over to the day of the wedding.

More than once in the past, because of the previous night's stag party, has a bridegroom been conducted to the altar by his friends, hardly fit to stand alone – and certainly not sufficiently in command of his senses to be able to follow the service in detail, or to make his vows in a proper spirit. The bride has found herself alone on her wedding night while her husband slept off the hangover from his stag party.

Probably, with such unfortunate results in mind, it has of recent years become the practice for most prospective bridegrooms to hold their stag parties some days in advance of the wedding, instead of on the night before it, leaving time for the after-effects to wear off and for the last minute arrangements for the wedding to be dealt with in an atmosphere of comparative sobriety.

A stag party is usually an informal affair, held in the local pub, a hotel, a restaurant or even in a night club – but wherever possible, a private room should be taken so that other guests will not be inconvenienced by the noise that is almost certain to arise.

Of course, the number of guests invited to the party will be related to the number of bachelor friends the bridegroom can claim – and to the amount of money it is felt people will want to afford. The latter point must also be taken into consideration when deciding on the place, the menu, if any, and the drinks and, in special circumstances, the entertainment to be provided. It is usual for stag party guests to pay their share of the total costs and the best man should take charge of the financial details, making sure that the bill is paid including an appropriate tip and that he collects the shares from all the invitees. The bridegroom may decide to contribute by, for example, paying for all the pre-meal drinks (which can come to a fair sum) but if he does so the best man will make sure that all the others pay for his meal by including it in with their shares. Before deciding on any extravagant entertainment therefore have a thought for what the poorest guest may like to pay and remember to warn people in round figures what they will be in for.

Among the invited guests will be the brothers of both the bride and the groom, providing, of course, that they are old enough. It is generally accepted that 17 is the lower age limit, though 18 is more realistic in view of the Liquor Licensing Laws which prohibits the supplying of alcoholic beverages to anyone below that age.

Formal invitations are quite unnecessary; a 'phone call or a verbal invitation when the bridegroom happens to meet his friends, is sufficient. Dinner jackets may be worn – if all the guests possess one. However, informal dress is more common nowadays.

The bridegroom is expected to arrive first at his party, in company with, or followed almost at once by, his best man. This allows the groom to greet his guests as they arrive while the best man dispenses, or suggests, the first round of drinks.

Of course, there will be no ladies among the guests and traditionally the party is restricted to unmarried men; however most people nowadays ignore the second restriction – and as it is the bridegroom's party, who can deny him the right to stretch convention as much as he likes?

The whole affair is traditionally ignored by the bride, treated with amused though shy interest by the sisters of the couple and girls of their age group, and with delighted laughter by the male relatives of an older generation, as they recall their own stag parties!

After the meal only two speeches are called for – though others may follow according to the humour and the inventiveness of the guests. Sometimes no speeches are made but the best man or the bridegroom will set the ball rolling by telling a naughty story or two, inviting others to contribute stories thereafter.

The first of the speeches, if any, should come from the best man, who can be expected to speak humorously and perhaps mock-lugubriously of the fond farewell they must make to yet another deserter from the happy ranks of the unattached males – another bachelor who has succumbed to feminine wiles, and who is about to embark upon the stormy seas of matrimony. A man who was once a man, but who is now to be shackled to a washing machine and a woman's apron strings. A being who is to be forbidden the comfort of an evening pint of the best at the local and rationed to a once weekly half pint of the cheapest brew – unless accompanied by his wife.

The best man may make use of some further points in his speech based on his personal knowledge of the groom.

An event or two during their schooldays.
The girls – unnamed – whom he is about to abandon.
How the cunning witch laid the trap to ensnare him.

The speech should not be too long; a good dinner and a few drinks will mellow the listeners, but make them outspoken if they get bored.

The bridegroom responds with an equally farcial farewell to his bachelor friends – friends whom he is glad to abandon because of their shockingly selfish way of life; a bunch of reprobates, boozers and ill-mannered oafs. How he is about to enjoy the salubrious company of somebody who will cook for him, warm his slippers, sew his buttons on and wash the car for him. Somebody who will pander to his merest whim. The home he will enjoy while his erstwhile friends are tramping the rain-drenched streets in search of company.

The bridegroom can extend his speech, always in a humorous vein, to bring in:

A sad farewell to his past girlfriends.

A welcome at his home for all his men friends – so long as they wipe their shoes on the doormat.

A request that financial aid should not be withheld if they ever again meet in a pub.

If there is to be an entertainment, it should be confined to a single act. Perhaps a cross-talk comedian, a ventriloquist, or a pianist to lead them all into a few songs, or – provided the bride is not likely to be upset to hear about it – a female entertainer may be engaged.

A wise best man will make sure that no-one needs to leave the party driving his own car. Girlfriends or wives can usually be persuaded to collect at an allotted hour or taxis can be arranged.

9

WHO DOES WHAT?

One of the earliest tasks of the bride and the bridegroom is to choose who are to be their helpers before, during and immediately after their wedding.

The matter needs careful thought if jealousies are not to be aroused. Relations often feel that they have a claim to be more than guests at a wedding; long-standing friends expect similar privileges – and not one of them may be suited to the particular duties involved.

Possibly he who considers himself most entitled to the office of best man is debarred because he has too little time to spare before the wedding, perhaps because he knows so few of the people concerned and would, in consequence, make a poor marshal, and not improbably because, however sincere he may be, he may lack the flair for organisation, the capacity to take charge of a situation, or be quick-witted enough to deal with an emergency.

Equally, an 'anxious-to-be' bridesmaid may not be led to understand that she is the 'one-too-many' of the girls who can hope to be invited to join the bridal procession. Maybe, too, her lack of composure would be likely to cause embarrassment during the ceremony, or possibly she has been excluded because her ability to remain standing on her feet throughout the service is in doubt – or even because her height just cannot be matched to that of any other suitable girl.

Others, of course, have duties which are inescapable. The need for the bride's father to be present at the church to give her away, for instance, is almost obligatory. Only where he is either dead or physically incapable of attending the service should a deputy be appointed.

The Chief Bridesmaid

It is quite usual for the bride to seek the help of her eldest unmarried sister as her chief bridesmaid, or, if she has no sister, another unmarried relative or her best unmarried friend.

There is no bounden duty laid on the bride to make such a choice if she considers another unmarried relative or friend temperamentally more suitable – but the alternative selection should not be made lightly and the unmarried sister or best friend who has been passed over should be told by the bride herself the reason for her decision, in the hope that goodwill and harmony will not be jeopardized.

The chief bridesmaid's duties are concerned mainly with two things; personal attention to the bride and the marshalling of the bridesmaids and pages.

She might be expected to help the bride to choose the bridesmaids' dresses, to rehearse them in their duties and to take charge of the bride's bouquet during the service.

She might be called upon to help dress the bride for her wedding, though this task is usually claimed by the bride's mother as a last service to her daughter. In any event, the chief bridesmaid will have enough to do to dress herself and to see to it that the bridesmaids are properly dressed for the occasion; their head-dresses, their posies, their shoes and the correct hang of their dresses – not to mention their arrival at the church well in advance of the bride.

During the service, the chief bridesmaid's station is immediately behind the bride and the bride's father. She will follow them in procession to the chancel steps and then, passing her own bouquet to the nearest bridesmaid, she will take the bridal bouquet and draw the bride's veil clear of her face.

When the newly-wed couple follow the clergyman into the vestry for the formality of signing the register, she and the best man follow immediately behind them.

Often, the chief bridesmaid (if she is of age) and the best man are chosen to sign the register as witnesses of the marriage.

The chief bridesmaid should be available to the bride during the reception, to smooth away any little worries or difficulties that may arise – often in consultation with the best man. And her final duty is to help the bride into her 'going away' outfit if she is needed, and to see her to her car.

The Bridesmaids

The bridesmaids are chosen by the bride from amongst her young relatives and friends – not forgetting those of the bridegroom. They generally number two or four, though for important weddings the numbers may rise as high as six or even eight. They need not all be girls; young boys as pages may be included. Pages are always very young; 5 to 8 years of age being the most acceptable limits – although there is nothing mandatory about it. They are nearly always young brothers of the couple or nephews. It is worth remembering that while a very small bridesmaid may look adorable, she is going to find standing still without talking during the service very difficult, and it is common sense to choose a child of an age that can understand what is required, and what is going on.

The bride almost always tries to match the bridesmaids and pages for size, sometimes a difficult task but making a most attractive picture when she has been successful. It is the bride's prerogative too to choose the material and pattern for the bridesmaids' dresses – and the pages' outfits. This includes the whole ensemble.

By tradition, the mothers of the bridesmaids each pay for their daughter's attire – an expensive business if the bride's choice happens to be ambitious. Hopefully they will be used as party dresses afterwards.

The bride should take care not to invite anyone to act as her bridesmaid whose parents would be unlikely to welcome the expense – unless as is sometimes the case, the bride's parents will provide the whole of the ensemble for each of the bridesmaids.

Whoever pays for the dresses and the accessories, it is usual to allow the bridesmaids to keep them after the wedding unless they are hired. Most large department stores have a bridal department where there is a wide range of bridal gowns, veils, head dresses and bridesmaids dresses to choose from. Alternatively, a good dressmaker could prove of immense help in deciding on the ensemble; she will advise too, on what is suitable for the time of the year, the fashionable styles and have a sense of matching colours, and of trimmings that will enhance the group as a whole.

She will be able to make suggestions concerning the modern trend in head-dresses; be that hats, haloes, tiaras or bows. She will know, too, whether or not a veil should be worn by the bride and even be able to advise on the most suitable posies or flower baskets to match or contrast with the dresses. There are also brides magazines which are full of current trends and ideas.

The duties of the bridesmaids and pages are to assist the bride from the moment she arrives at the church for her wedding until she finally leaves the reception on the first stage of her honeymoon.

'Assist' is hardly the word as far as the wedding ceremony is concerned; the bridesmaids and pages are merely decorative in the procession and have no other duties than tending the bridal train – if it should be long enough to require attention.

In the procession they follow in pairs behind the bride, the pages leading and the taller or older bridesmaids coming last.

At the reception afterwards, the bridesmaids might be expected to carry around the portions of the wedding cake, at the proper time, and offer them to the guests – but after that their duties are complete and they can enjoy themselves for the rest of the day as each of them sees fit.

Matron of Honour

There is no absolute need for a bride to be attended by a retinue of bridesmaids. Sometimes it may be that she has no young female relatives or, indeed, any suitable young friends available. This often happens if the bride is new to the district, or has travelled some considerable distance to marry.

Sometimes, too, the bride may be older and young bridesmaids may be out of place; or it may even be that she is most anxious to ask some particular woman to attend her who happens to be married, especially her sisters.

In all such cases it is quite usual for the bride to be attended by a matron of honour. The lady chosen will be a married woman and she will be the only attendant, acting as the chief – and only – bridesmaid.

Her duties are identical with those of a chief bridesmaid, but she will not wear the finery.

In such cases the bride, too, usually abandons the full wedding dress and veil for an outfit similar to that worn by her matron of honour – though this is by no means a must.

The Bride's Mother

The bride's mother is one of those who have inescapable duties to perform in connection with her daughter's wedding – unless, of course, she happens to be incapacitated when her mantle will fall on the bride's oldest sister if she has one, or an aunt or even a grandmother.

Yet, despite the fact that she will probably have to work harder than anyone else to make for the success of the occasion, the bride's mother will have almost no official part in the wedding itself.

She will carry the whole of the responsibility for the social side of the event and as the hostess she will issue the invitations to the wedding guests both to the ceremony and to the reception afterwards. She will need to exercise a great deal of tact, too, to include as far as possible the guests suggested by the bridegroom's parents, bearing in mind that her husband will be expected to pay the bills!

The bride's mother will be deeply concerned in helping to choose the bridal gown and no doubt her advice will be sought concerning the bridesmaid's dresses.

Among the other cares she must shoulder are:

1. The choosing, printing and despatching of the invitations.

2. The press announcements.

3. The printing of the Order of Service as arranged between the couple and the clergyman.

4. The church decorations.

5. The wedding bouquets, buttonholes and corsages for the two mothers – in consultation with the bride to make sure that they are in harmony with the *tout ensemble*.

6. Ordering the wedding cars to take the bride and her father, the bridesmaids, and of course herself to the service. She will need to order, too, cars wanted by other guests – and to take everybody from the church to the reception afterwards. The only cars that will not require her attention are those that will carry the bridegroom and his best man to the church – and the 'going away' car for the bridal couple on the first stage of their honeymoon, which the bridegroom should arrange.

7. She will have to make or have made the wedding cake and the arrangements for its delivery to the reception.

8. The photographer needs to be booked. He will normally take photographs of the bride arriving with her father. Sometimes he is allowed to take photographs during parts of the service or during the signing of the register, but most photographs will be of the bride and groom with their bridesmaids and pages, their parents and other relatives after they have come out from the church. The photographer will, if the couple wish, take some black and white shots and, together with a form which includes all the relevant details

and will have been completed by the bride and groom, send one to the local newspaper who will print it free of charge at the editor's discretion. The photographer will also arrive at the reception before the guests to take the 'official' and 'pretend' photograph of cutting the cake. The cake has several tiers and this may be the only time to photograph it complete as many caterers take away the middle tier to cut it up during the reception. There are usually enough amateur photographers around to capture the actual cutting of the cake.

9. Arranging the details of the reception in consultation with the caterer and arranging where this is to be held, including:

    (a) The menu.
    (b) The wines.
    (c) The table decorations.
    (d) The seating arrangements.
    (e) Booking a private room for the bride where she can change into her 'going away' outfit.
    (f) Drawing up a table plan if needed.
    (g) Arranging the printing of place cards, menus, book matches, table napkins if this is desired.

10. The collection of what is left of the wedding cake after the reception; the cutting and boxing of the portions for posting to distant relatives and friends.

In certain areas there are firms who will do everything for the bride's mother from catering to car hire, flowers, photography, video recording, the wedding cake, entertainment, stationery, bridal wear and hire facilities.

As the wedding, in all probability, will take place in the district where the bride lives, her mother can expect to do some entertaining, in addition to the gathering of their friends and relatives at the reception. This will be particularly strenuous if the bridegroom, his family and friends come from any considerable distance.

As the hostess, the bride's mother may find herself involved in arranging hotel accommodation for some of her guests and may even feel duty bound to put some of the bridegroom's relatives up in her own home.

She will also find that her daughter will need her help in dressing for the wedding and though it is the duty of the chief bridesmaid to attend the bride, few mothers are willing to forego this last chore for their daughters.

She will then leave the bride at home with her father and make haste, probably alone, to reach the church ahead of her.

Her place during the marriage service is in the front row of pews, among her other children and perhaps her parents; on the bride's side of the aisle, to the left facing the altar.

She takes no part in the service until she is led by the bridegroom's father to the vestry to witness the signing of the marriage register. She comes out of the church on the left arm of the bridegroom's father following the pages and bridesmaids in procession with the bridegroom's mother and the bride's father behind them.

She and her husband then leave the church immediately after the newly-weds. They are the hosts at the reception and must, of course, be there first, in time to receive their guests.

The Bride's Father

The bride's father has the dual privilege of giving his daughter away at her wedding – and paying for the reception afterwards.

Often formally dressed in a morning coat, grey trousers, grey tie and sometimes a grey top hat – and wearing a buttonhole similar to that worn by the bridegroom and the best man – the bride's father escorts his daughter from their home to the church. If her father should happen to be dead or physically incapable of attending the wedding, the bride's eldest brother or male guardian, or uncle takes his place.

He arrives at the church with the bride after everyone else has gathered within – though it is bad form to keep the clergyman and the congregation waiting after the appointed time. Almost at once, with his daughter on his right arm, he will lead the procession towards the chancel steps.

At the proper time in the service, he will take his daughter's hand and give it to the clergyman in a gesture of giving her away.

After the service, the bride's father accompanies the bridegroom's mother into the vestry in the wake of the newly-weds, to see the final act of the marriage – the signing of the register.

Immediately after leaving the church, he will hurry with his wife to the venue of the reception where, as host and hostess, they greet their guests.

Finally, the bride's father may be called on by the best man, during the reception, to propose the toast of the 'Bride and Bridegroom'.

The Best Man

The best man is chosen by the bridegroom from amongst his relatives or friends who are usually unmarried, and in general, it is his closest companion that is honoured.

The duties are onerous and the bridegroom would be well advised to make his selection with extreme care. The best man will find himself a sort of master of ceremonies, the chief usher, the repository of valuables – such as the wedding ring and the certificate permitting the marriage, organiser-in-chief, toastmaster and paymaster. He is also likely to find himself the bridegroom's messenger boy, father confessor, persuader, remembrancer, office boy and valet.

Obviously he must have a flair for organisation, a steady nerve, be a good mixer and have limitless tact.

His many duties include:

1. Taking the bridegroom to his wedding – on time.
2. Detailing the ushers to their duties.
3. Safeguarding the wedding ring until it is to be placed on the bride's finger.

4. After the service, accompanying the chief bridesmaid to the vestry, behind the bride and bridegroom. He and the chief bridesmaid are usually chosen as the two witnesses to sign the register – though this is not obligatory. Under the circumstances and to avoid confusion at the very last moment, it is well for the bride and bridegroom to decide and arrange, well in advance, who the official witnesses are to be.

5. He should follow the bride and groom out of the church with the chief bridesmaid and then be at the church door to usher the newly-weds to their places in front of the photographer and see them to their car for the journey to the reception. He then ushers the guests into their cars in turn – parents first, grandparents, uncles and aunts, bridesmaids and then the friends and more distant relatives.

6. He pays the marriage fees to the clergyman (or perhaps the verger), inclusive of the cost of the organist, the choir and bells, if this has not already been done.

7. At the reception he calls on the speakers and replies to the toast of 'The Bridesmaids' on their behalf.

8. He reads out the messages of congratulation that have been received.

9. He sees the couple into their car after the reception, ready for the start of their honeymoon journey, and hands over the various documents such as rail or air tickets, passports, traveller's cheques and route maps, which he has been safeguarding during the ceremony and the reception.

Other responsibilities include:

(a) Arranging a car to take him and the bridegroom to the church – and the 'going away' car or taxi for the newly-weds.

(b) Act as baggage master to the couple.

Though the best man is supposed to help the bridegroom to dress for his wedding, this is hardly necessary with modern clothes. In the picturesque days of the Prince Regent, of course, with the magnificent velvets, silks and satins worn by the bridegrooms; socks, stockings and shoe buckles; the best man needed the services of a valet to help him dress the nervous buck – and many an hour to spare for the purpose.

Today, the best man usually arrives at the bridegroom's home as he is dressing; collects the wedding ring, identifies the baggage, takes charge of the keys, the various tickets and other documents needed for the honeymoon and the cash necessary to pay the marriage fees at the church – checks that nothing has been forgotten – and even then he will probably find that the nervous bridegroom has neglected to provide himself with a pair of black socks or has broken a shoelace and there isn't a spare!

The best man should have collected buttonholes for the bridegroom and himself. Once he and the bridegroom are ready there is nothing for it but to watch the clock and worry about the taxi arriving on time. Nothing could make a more embarrassing start to a wedding than for the bridegroom to arrive at the church after his bride!

And from then on he continually fingers the ring in his waistcoat pocket, knowing that though he would be by no means the first best man to forget it, his failure to produce it at the right moment might constitute a disaster.

The best man's clothes are similar to those worn by the bridegroom. A morning coat, grey trousers and grey tie – though if the wedding is less formal, both might wear lounge suits. The one item that may not be omitted is a buttonhole. It is usual for the groom and best man and the two fathers to have the same buttonholes; white, red, pink or yellow carnations, or roses, while the ushers all have white or red buttonholes. But it is equally possible for the groom to have a buttonhole to harmonise with his suit. The choice is usually the bride's who will order all the flowers with her mother.

Ushers

The ushers are chosen by the bridegroom, generally in consultation with his best man, from amongst the unmarried brothers and friends of his own, and of his bride.

Four are sufficient – unless there is a very long list of guests to be seated in the church.

The ushers must, of course, arrive first at the church and as the guests appear, they hand them their Order of Service sheets and conduct them to their seats. Relatives and friends of the bride sit in the pews on the left of the aisle facing the chancel steps, and those of the bridegroom, on the right – the immediate families of the bride and bridegroom being placed in the front pews on their respective sides of the aisle.

Obviously, it is better to choose ushers who know most of the guests and who will have less need to ask them if they are 'friends of the bride or the bridegroom?'

Dress for the ushers should be similar to that worn by the bridegroom and the best man; morning coats, grey trousers and a wedding tie, or dark lounge suits. Buttonholes, usually of carnations, are worn in their coat lapels.

Moss Bros., of Covent Garden, London, WC2, are renowned for their hire service in wedding clothes for men and women. They have branches throughout Britain and they also do a postal service from London.

I give fuller details for the best man than space allows in this book in 'The Best Man's Duties', a companion book in the *paperfront* series.

10

ANNOUNCEMENTS AND SENDING OUT THE INVITATIONS

The first public proclamation of the forthcoming wedding is made at the time of the engagement of the couple. Such announcements receive much less attention than they did some years ago, and, in fact, there is no longer any absolute need to have the event published in the press at all.

However, there are occasions when an announcement in the advertisement columns of the press is of value to the newly engaged couple – particularly to those who have a very wide circle of friends and acquaintances. In such instances it might well be impracticable to write a letter to every one of them.

Sometimes, too, it might be that one or other of the couple or one of their parents happens to be a figure of national importance or of wide public interest – a politician or a pop-singer, perhaps – making the announcement a matter of public concern. Any such announcements, of course, would be enough to bring the reporters and photographers flocking to the door, on the instant!

In such cases, and where friends and relatives of the couple are widely scattered over the country, the announcements should be made in one or more of the national daily newspapers, where a wide circulation is assured. *The Times, The Daily Telegraph* and *The Guardian*, the *Scotsman* and

Glasgow Herald are five which spring to mind at once, as publishing special announcement columns.

If it happens, however, that the friends and relatives are fairly tightly domiciled in a single large city or county, the local newspaper is the best medium – and, of course, is considerably less expensive – in which to advertise than in the national morning newspapers. If the bride and bridegroom do happen to live in districts distant from one another, it might be wise to use the press of each locality in which to proclaim the betrothal and the forthcoming wedding.

The advertisement should be sent to the Classified Advertisements Manager of the newspapers concerned, and they should be drafted in the following manner to appear under 'Forthcoming Marriages'.

Mr. P.J. Fry and Miss A. Lloyd

The engagement is announced between Peter John Fry, only son of Mr. and Mrs. G.H. Fry of Esher, Surrey and Ann, younger daughter of Col. and Mrs. L.R. Lloyd of Horsham, West Sussex.

It could be varied to read:

The marriage has been arranged and will take place shortly between Peter, only son of Mr. and Mrs. G.H. Fry of Esher, Surrey, and Ann, younger daughter of Col. and Mrs. L.R. Lloyd of Horsham, West Sussex.

If, however, the bridegroom has a title or carries a military rank, the wording to the announcement would more probably be as follows:

Flight Lieut. P.J. Fry and Miss A. Lloyd

The engagement is announced between Flight Lieutenant Peter John Fry, A.F.C., R.A.F., only son of Mr. and Mrs.

G.H. Fry of Esher, Surrey and Ann, young daughter of Col. and Mrs. L.R. Lloyd of Horsham, West Sussex.

More people are using their local newspapers to announce engagements and these normally appear under the 'Births, Marriages and Deaths' columns. They tend to be less formal and would read as follows:

LLOYD-FRY – Mr. and Mrs. Robert Lloyd of Horsham are pleased to announce the engagement of their eldest daughter, Ann, to Peter, second son of Mr. and Mrs. G.H. Fry of Esher, Surrey.

If it should be that the bride's father is dead, the last sentence of the announcement should read:

... and Ann, younger daughter of the late Col. L.R. Lloyd and Mrs. Lloyd of Horsham, West Sussex.

If it is the bride's mother who has died, the sentence will read:

... and Ann, younger daughter of Col. L.R. Lloyd and the late Mrs. Lloyd of Horsham, West Sussex.

If the bride's parents have been divorced, the address of each of them should be given, as follows:

... and Ann, younger daughter of Col. L.R. Lloyd of Horsham, West Sussex and Mrs. R.L. Lloyd of Guildford, Surrey.

If the parents have been divorced and the bride's mother has re-married, the announcement should conclude:

... and Ann, younger daugher of Col. L.R. Lloyd of Horsham, West Sussex and Mrs. C.B. Brooklyn of Coldharbour, Surrey.

If it is the bridegroom's parents who are either dead or have been divorced, precisely the same amendment to the announcement should be made in the first sentence, as would be made in the last sentence, where the bride was concerned.

In due course invitations to the wedding and the reception need to be printed and despatched by post to those for whom they are intended. The list is a matter for the bride's parents – as hosts, they must select their guests. But it is common and much kinder for the two sets of parents and the engaged couple to consult one another on the subject.

It is reasonable to assume that both the bride and the bridegroom – and their parents – will wish to invite similar numbers from amongst their own relatives and friends – though this is not necessarily the case. For instance, a bridegroom may come from some considerable distance to his wedding; a distance not easily covered by all his friends. Or perhaps the bride is a member of some society which might bring her an unusually large number of friends.

In any event, the bride's parents must be left to make the final decision as to numbers to be invited – at least as far as the reception is concerned; they will be expected to pay the bill for the whole of the entertainment and it could well be an embarrassing amount, although it is becoming more common for both families to share the cost and even for the bride and bridegroom to make a contribution.

It is possible to issue separate invitations to the wedding ceremony and the reception afterwards with a register office wedding but it is more usual to combine the invitations on a single card – unless, of course, there is to be a large discrepancy between the numbers invited to attend the ceremony and those expected to be present at the reception later.

Invitations should be sent out well in advance of the event; probably as much as six weeks before the wedding, so as to give the guests plenty of time to complete their own arrangements and to decline any alternative invitations they may receive to other functions on the same day and at the same time.

The invitations can be printed in a standard fashion, leaving the sender to fill in the names and addresses in the appropriate places.

Any good stationers (such as W.H. Smith shops) or printers will be able to show you a wide range of wedding stationery to choose from. These include invitations (including those with a tear off reply slip); Order of Service sheets; menu cards; place cards; serviettes and rings; book matches; ashtrays and drip mats with the bride and groom's Christian names and the wedding date. Stationers will also provide the boxes and cards for sending wedding cake to those unable to attend.

A very popular format is:

> *Colonel and Mrs. Leslie R. White*
> *request the pleasure of the company of*
>
> ....
> *at the marriage of their daughter*
>
> *Ann*
> *with*
> *Mr. Peter John Green*
> *at St. George's Parish Church, Ashford*
> *on Saturday, 20th April, 19XX*
> *at 11 a.m.*
> *and at a reception afterwards at the*
> *Carlton Hotel.*

12 Fir Tree Lane,
Ashford,
Kent.   *R.S.V.P.*

Of course, the first line of the invitation will vary with the status of those sending the invitation.

If the bride's mother is dead, it will read:

> *Colonel Leslie R. White*
> *requests the pleasure . . .*

If it is the father who is dead, it will read:

> *Mrs. Joan R. White*
> *requests the pleasure . . .*

If the bride's parents are divorced the invitation should read:

> *Colonel Leslie R. White and Mrs. Joan Bodkin*
> *request the pleasure . . .*

Invitations to a register office wedding are similar and would read:

> *Mr. and Mrs. A.B. Cox*
> *request the pleasure of*
>
> ....
> *at the marriage of their daughter*
> *Jane*
> *with*
> *Mr. James Brown*
> *at the Register Office, Park Road*
> *on Thursday, 10th May, 19XX*
> *11.30 a.m.*
> *and at a reception afterwards at the*
> *Royal Hotel.*

12 Dorset Street,
Weymouth,
Dorset.   *R.S.V.P.*

And if both parents are dead, the invitations will be issued in the names of the guardians or relatives who are to act as hosts for the occasion.

The R.S.V.P. is most necessary, as the hostess must know in advance how many guests she may expect – especially for the meal at the reception.

Replies should be brief, despatched without delay and couched in the third person, such as:

> 15 Winsgrove Terrace,
> Ellesmere.

Mr. and Mrs. Joseph Fleet and their daughter, Phyllis, thank Colonel and Mrs. Leslie R. White for their kind invitation to their daughter's wedding at St. George's Parish Church on Saturday, 20th April, 19XX at 11 a.m. and to a reception afterwards at the Carlton Hotel, and are most happy to accept.

11th March, 19XX

Such a note requires no signature.

If it is impossible to accept the invitation, either because of a prior engagement or for some private family reason, it is a matter of courtesy both to acknowledge the invitation, and to make your decision not to attend clear.

The refusal should be as brief as the acceptance and similarly written in the third person, though an excuse might be added, however vague it may appear to be:

> 15 Winsgrove Terrace,
> Ellesmere.

Mr. and Mrs. Joseph Fleet and their daughter, Phyllis, thank Colonel and Mrs. Leslie R. White for their kind invitation to their daughter's wedding at St. George's Parish Church on Saturday, 20th April, 19XX and to the reception afterwards.

Unfortunately they have accepted a prior engagement for that date and must therefore decline with regret.

11th March, 19XX

And again, no signature is required.

There are occasions, when the invitations to the wedding outstrips the ability of the hosts to entertain at the reception afterwards. This may be because of the expense, or it may have been brought about by a recent bereavement, which has decided the bride and her parents to restrict the celebrations to a small, private gathering of the two families and perhaps a few of their close friends.

In neither case is there any need for the bride's parents to limit the numbers they invite to the church, but it is usual then to omit all mention of the reception on the invitation cards.

Where the wedding service is a small family affair and a reception is to be held to include other guests who were not at the ceremony the invitation would read:

> *Mr. and Mrs. J.S. White*
> *request the pleasure of the company of*
>
> ....
>
> *on the evening of the wedding*
> *of their daughter*
> *Maria*
> *with*
> *Mr. Peter J. Green*
> *at The Park Hotel, King's Road*
> *at 7.30 p.m.*
> *on Friday, 7th May, 19XX*

12 Fir Tree Lane,
Woodhouse.   *R.S.V.P.*

An alternative form is:

> *Mr. and Mrs. J.S. White*
> *request the pleasure of the company of*
>
> ....
>
> *at an evening reception*
> *at The Royal Hotel, The Mall*
> *at 7 p.m.*
> *to celebrate the marriage of their daughter*
> *Susan*
> *with*
> *Mr. George Black*
> *on Saturday, 30th April, 19XX*

12 Fir Tree Lane,
Woodhouse.   *R.S.V.P.*

Sometimes invitations already accepted must be declined, possibly because of illness, an accident, or even through a sudden death in the family. In such a case the bride's parents should be informed at once. It may give them time to amend the numbers given to the caterers. A simple note is all that is necessary; perhaps:

> *15 Winsgrove Terrace,*
> *Ellesmere.*

Mr. and Mrs. Fleet and their daughter, Phyllis, sincerely regret the necessity, because of a bereavement in the family, to have to inform you that they will now be unable to attend your daughter's wedding on 20th April 19XX or the reception afterwards.

21st March, 19XX

Again, there is no need for a signature.

The day after the wedding a press announcement can appear under the 'Marriages' column. The most usual wording is as follows:

Mr. P.J. Green and Miss A. White

The marriage took place on 20th April at the Church of St. George, Woodhouse, of Mr. Peter J. Green, only son of Mr. and Mrs. A.F. Green of Esher, Surrey and Miss Ann White, elder daughter of Mr. and Mrs. J.F. White of Tonbridge, Kent.

Where one party has been divorced the wording could be:

Mr. P.J. Green and Miss A. White

A service of blessing was held yesterday at the Church of St. Mark, Balham after the marriage of Mr. Peter Green, only son of Mr. and Mrs. A.F. Green of Esher, Surrey and Miss Ann White, elder daughter of Mr. and Mrs. J.F. White of Tonbridge, Kent. The Rev. J.M. Graham officiated.

Or the wording can be simpler:

Mr. P.J. Green and Miss A. White

The marriage took place quietly in Baldock on 20th April between Mr. Peter J. Green and Miss Ann White.

11

THE ENGAGEMENT RING
AND THE WEDDING GIFTS

The engagement ring is perhaps the first serious token of affection from a prospective bridegroom to his future wife, but as this is more in the nature of a seal to a contract between them, it can hardly be classed as a 'present'.

Other gifts from a bridegroom to his bride will obviously follow between their engagement and the wedding – but there are certain things that should be observed in this connection. He should not buy expensive items such as jewellery or furs; or any item that could suggest that he was 'keeping' her.

The bride, in return, should not occupy any home that the bridegroom has bought or procured, in advance of the wedding; nor should she make use of any furniture, linen or any other articles that have been bought for their joint use in their new home.

It is quite usual for the bride to give her future husband an engagement present; a signet ring is popular, a gold chain, a tie pin or cuff links are also common gifts.

Soon after the invitations to the wedding have been sent out, presents will begin to arrive for the betrothed couple from relatives and friends. Such offerings should always be addressed to the bride at her home and not to the bridegroom – even though it may happen that the donor has never even met the bride!

The presents may vary from the decorative to the

practical, from the purely personal to the 'homey' and from the very expensive to the intrinsically valueless. Yet whatever the value or the nature of the gift, each will be as well-intended as any other, each will assuredly be given as an expression of well-wishing and each probably in accordance with its donor's means.

Although there are those who feel it bad taste, the majority of couples will spend some time compiling a gift list so that when friends telephone to find out what the couple would like as a wedding present they can be given several ideas or even sent a copy of the list.

If a list is to be made out it should be specific – giving the product, the manufacturer, the style, colour, etc., and where it is obtainable. The following outline list may help you decide some of the items you will need for your home:

Living Room	Bedroom	Bathroom
Clock	Pillows	Towels
Cushions	Duvet	Bath mat
Nest of tables	Sheets	Mirror
Lamps	Duvet covers	Linen basket
Music centre	Blankets	Bath rack
Television set	Pillow cases	Indoor clothes line
Vases	Bedspread	Bathroom scales
Chairs	Bedside clock/tea	Towel rail
Rugs	maker	
Settee	Electric blanket	Soap holder

Kitchen	Dining Room	Miscellaneous
Refrigerator/freezer	Dining table	Vacuum cleaner
Washing machine	Dining chairs	Carpet sweeper
Dish washer	Place mats	Brushes & mops
Cooker	Tablecloths	Dustpan & brush
Food mixer	Trolley	Garden furniture

Kitchen	*Dining Room*	*Miscellaneous*
Electric kettle	Dinner service	Garden tools
Coffee percolator	Tea service	Wastepaper baskets
Kitchen knives	Breakfast set	Mower
Bread board	Salt & pepper mills	Luggage
Bread bin	Fruit bowl	Car rug
Electric toaster	Cutlery	Picnic set
Slow cooker	Water jug &	Ornaments
Microwave oven	tumblers	Wine rack
Sandwich maker	Wine glasses	Shrubs & trees
Mixing bowls	Sherry glasses	
Saucepans	Decanters	
Tea towels	Sideboard	
Can opener	Cheese board &	
Kitchen tools	knife	
Kitchen scales	Hot plate	
Pressure cooker	Candlesticks	
Storage jars		
Trays		
Wooden spoons		
Pedal bin		
Washing up bowl		
Casserole set		
Frying pan		
Oven gloves		
Spice rack		

Cheques are often more useful to a newly-married couple who will have a hundred and one needs before they complete their home – but except in the case of fathers, it is not the kind of present that can be suggested with propriety by the bride or her bridegroom.

Occasionally, arrangements can be made for the display of the wedding presents at the reception, but more often the couple arrange to show their presents either in their new home, or at the bride's home, and cards can be printed as follows:

Dear . . . .

We would like to express our sincere thanks for your kind wishes and most acceptable gift.

Would you please come to our Show of Presents on Wednesday, 17th September at 7.30 p.m.

Joan and Eric

(Telephone number)

12 Avenue Road,
Stockwell.

Such an exhibition can be made most attractive; white tablecloths and tiers of boxes underneath can do much to set off the beauty and interest of the collection of items. Each present should have a card sent with it so that it may stand beside the piece on the display tables, giving the donor's name and address. In the case of cheques, only an envelope is displayed stating the name and address of the donor but giving no information concerning its value. Under no circumstances should the cheque itself be displayed. It should be paid into the bank!

A similar restriction should be placed on less usual presents, such as an insurance policy, the deeds of a house or a shares certificate. Envelopes should represent the items on the display tables, endorsed with the words 'Insurance Policy', 'Deeds of House', or 'Shares Certificate' – and the name and address of the donor.

After the reception the bride's parents should remove any show of presents to their own home, where a suitable display can again be arranged for the benefit of friends and neighbours who did not attend the reception. This display may well last until a few days before the end of the newly-married couple's honeymoon, when her mother and father can take the gifts to the new home on their daughter and son-in-law's return.

After the honeymoon it is the bride's duty to write and thank the individual donors of presents. Such letters should be sent out almost as soon as she takes up her residence in her new home, but where the numbers make the task a lengthy one, a verbal, even a telephone, message will serve as an interim measure. However close the giver and however fulsome the verbal thanks, a letter in due course is a must.

There is a certain amount of tradition to be observed in the sending of wedding presents:

(a) Relatives should send a present whether or not they attend the reception and the wedding – so long as they have been invited.

(b) All those attending the wedding ceremony and the reception afterwards are expected to send a present.

(c) There is no need for a friend to send a present when the invitation has been declined – though it is usual to do so when the cause is illness or some other reason that, if it had not arisen, would not have meant a refusal.

(d) There is no need to send a present where the invitation is to the wedding ceremony only – and does not include the reception afterwards.

(e) All presents should be sent to the bride at her parents' home, before the wedding – where they are sent afterwards, they should be addressed to both the bride and the bridegroom at their new home.

(f) Once in a while, though rarely, a present is intended for the bridegroom only. In such a case it should be sent to his parents' address and be acknowledged by him after the honeymoon. It may be displayed with the other presents.

(g) If a present is received, it is good manners to invite the giver to the wedding ceremony and usually, though not necessarily, to the reception afterwards. To avoid any embarrassment on this score, it is best to wait until invitations to the wedding and the reception have been received before sending presents.

It is common practice for the bridegroom to present each of the bridesmaids with a small present either before the wedding or during the reception. A small gift such as a silver chain with a pendant or a locket or a necklace is suitable. If there are any pages, they should not be overlooked – a plaything is generally most suitable.

12

THE CEREMONY

Church of England

A Clergyman of the Church of England may not refuse to perform a marriage service so long as he is sure that there is no legal or ecclesiastical objection to it – and indeed, he must satisfy himself that the law does in fact specifically permit each particular marriage, as to make a knowingly false declaration is a criminal offence.

In the case of the re-marriage of a divorced person, while it may be in order under civil law, ecclesiastical or church authority forbids the re-marriage of divorced persons in church. Some clergy are prepared to follow the civil law.

Where a clergyman follows ecclesiastical authority he may conduct a service of blessing following a civil wedding. This must not pretend to be a wedding and there are no legal formalities. This service of blessing can be held in a church, or before the reception at the bride's home, in a marquee, hotel or hired hall, if the clergyman is willing to officiate.

Any day of the week may be chosen by the couple as their wedding day, including Sundays and even Good Friday – though of course it is necessary for them to consult the clergyman concerned to make sure that it is convenient to him. However, the church does discourage weddings during Lent.

The popular days for such happy occasions are Fridays and Saturdays, both because it probably gives the couple an extra weekend for their honeymoon and because it is generally more convenient for their guests. Saturday mornings usually result in a queue of wedding parties at most churches and those who wish to marry at such a time on that day should talk to the clergyman of the church about it well in advance of the projected date. Generally months ahead.

Times preferred are between 11 a.m. and 4 p.m. – leaving plenty of time for the reception afterwards.

When the couple have decided on a church they should make an appointment to see the clergyman. Very often he will suggest that they attend a marriage preparation course and, among other things, will discuss what form the service will take.

With the Alternative Service Book 1980, those who wish to be unconventional are given much greater scope by this new service, but it can also be conducted in a very traditional manner. The bridal procession and the ceremony of giving away are optional, and full provision is made for the marriage to take place during a service of Holy Communion.

Two sets of vows are included (with or without the promise to 'obey') which the couple may choose to read instead of repeating after the clergyman. During the vows the bride and groom face each other, and words are provided for the bride either after receiving the ring or on giving a ring to the bridegroom.

The service may incorporate prayers which the couple have written or selected in co-operation with the clergyman and they may choose an appropriate reading or readings from the Bible.

During the scripture reading and sermon the bride and bridegroom may sit in chairs that have been specially placed for them.

The service can be tailored to suit the particular couple involved so that much of the detail will be decided in consultation with the officiating clergyman.

Also well in advance, the clergyman should be consulted about the decoration of his church. White flowers and greenery are usual for weddings but coloured flower arrangements are now very popular, often to match or enhance the bridesmaids' dresses. Lilies, roses, carnations, chrysanthemums, and dahlias are used – with perhaps ferns or evergreens. A vast display is quite unnecessary – and any good florist will do the whole thing for you, or perhaps members of the church flower committee.

A decision has to be made in advance too, concerning the music for the service and it is well to have a talk with the organist as soon as possible. Though it is accepted that it is the bride's prerogative to choose the hymns and, of course, a wedding march, it is obvious that the clergyman and organist's advice should be taken fully into account.

This is particularly applicable where a choir is needed.

From this point it is possible to arrange the full details of the service on a printed sheet, known as the 'Order of Service'. And if the bridal couple and the bride's mother complete all these arrangements in good time, it is possible to have the Order of Service printed for the use of all concerned.

On the morning of the wedding the excitement rises. At an early hour the bride will start dressing with her mother's help; the bridegroom will dress too, though less formally, while the bridesmaids and the guests prepare less hastily in their own homes.

An hour before the wedding is due to start, the chief bridesmaid should arrive at the bride's home – dressed and all ready. She will then help the bride to finish her dressing whilst the bride's mother snatches an opportunity to don her wedding attire.

At about the same time the best man should arrive, dressed for the ceremony, at the bridegroom's home.

Also at about the same time, the bridesmaids will begin to congregate at the bride's home while the ushers make ready individually in their own homes, for the service.

At least half an hour before the ceremony is due to start, the head usher or groomsman must arrive at the church. Immediately afterwards the other ushers are due and should then receive their final instructions from him,

The head usher will delegate several ushers to direct cars and help them park if necessary. Others will be asked to meet guests at the church door, hand out Order of Service sheets, and conduct the guests to their pews. He will remind them that the bride's mother, brothers and sisters and her grandparents should be seated in the front pew to the left of the nave facing the altar.

Others of the bride's relatives and friends should be seated on the same side of the church in descending order of relationship and closeness of friendship – so far as is conveniently possible – from the pews immediately behind the bride's mother to the back of the church.

Similarly, the bridegroom's relatives and friends will occupy the pews on the right of the nave. Part of the front row on that side may be needed for the groom and best man before the service and for the best man when the bride and groom go to the altar, so the closer members of his family may have to go in the pews immediately behind.

As a last instruction, the head usher will hand over copies of the Order of Service to the ushers, either to lay in the pews in advance, or more usually, to hand out as they conduct the wedding party and the guests to their seats.

Meanwhile, the best man should be making quite certain that the bridegroom is properly dressed for his wedding. He should also check the items he must take with him – the wedding ring or rings in his waistcoat pocket, money in his hip pocket to pay the marriage fees if they have not been paid at the time of a rehearsal and the couple's rail, boat or air tickets, passports and hotel reservations in his inside pocket.

Fifteen minutes before the service is due to start, he should conduct the bridegroom to the church and they then usually find themselves some secluded spot in which to wait. The clergyman often takes this opportunity to check details for the register.

From about now on, the guests begin to arrive and must be conducted to their seats. Those who have not met for some time, and those who are meeting for the first time, will be inclined to chat at the church door, causing a little obstruction and possibly creating a hold-up when the bride arrives. A little gentle hint here and there should get them to their places in ample time, however.

The chief bridesmaid should arrive in company with the other bridesmaids and the pages, not less than five minutes before the bride is due. They should gather in the church porch ready to form a procession and again, though the guests will tend to stop and talk to them, they should be dissuaded as much as possible as time will be getting short.

At the time the bridesmaids arrive, the best man should lead the bridegroom along the nave to the chancel steps – the best man on the bridegroom's right, though often the groom and best man wait in the front pew until the first notes of the wedding march.

The arrival, entrance and bridal procession is one of the high spots of pageantry for the occasion and it is important therefore that everybody should be in their places in good time. And the bride must arrive on her father's arm exactly on time. They arrive at the church last and in modern traffic conditions it is well for them to leave home early, even if it means that they have to cruise around for a few minutes to adjust their arrival to the exactly scheduled time. Great panic can be caused by a bride who arrives early!

Nor must this be an occasion when the bride exercises a woman's right to be late. It would be discourteous to the clergyman, the organist and the guests – and besides, it may cause serious delay to someone else's wedding which may be due to take place immediately afterwards.

A few photographs may be taken as the bride walks towards the church on her father's arm. The chief bridesmaid should make any last-minute adjustments to the bride's dress.

The organist will be warned of the bride's arrival, and move over from the introductory music to the wedding march, and with his daughter on his right arm, her father will lead her forward into the body of the church, in slow time – the pages and the bridesmaids taking up their places in the

ALTAR

CHOIR STALLS

CHOIR STALLS

MINISTER

GROOM

BEST MAN

BRIDE'S FATHER

BRIDE

PEWS

PEWS

BRIDE'S

BRIDEGROOM'S

RELATIONS

RELATIONS

AND FRIENDS

AND FRIENDS

BRIDESMAIDS

1. The procession.

procession, in pairs with the chief bridesmaid just behind the bride and her father.

To effect a properly paced procession, the bride and her father should move off with the left foot in time with the march, those following picking up the step as they fall in behind.

The officiating clergyman and the choir will usually meet the bride at the door and precede her down the aisle or sometimes he may await the bride on the chancel steps.

The bridegroom and his best man should turn to welcome the bride as she approaches and her father should lead her to the bridegroom's left. As they face the altar and the clergyman, they stand from left to right – the bride's father, the bride, the bridegroom and the best man.

Once they are in position with the bridesmaids standing in pairs behind the bride, the chief bridesmaid should step forward just as her father releases her arm to take the bride's bouquet and set her veil clear of her face, back over her head. The chief bridesmaid then returns to her place immediately behind the bride, satisfying herself that the bridesmaids and pages are in their places too.

At this point a hymn is often sung. It gives the couple an opportunity to relax a little. The clergyman then begins the chosen service stating the reason for the gathering in the church, the reason for matrimony, followed by a demand to know if there is any impediment to the marriage, first from the congregation, and then from the couple. To guard against malicious allegations the clergyman may demand a bond from anyone alleging impediment.

If he is satisfied that there is no legal objection to the union, he will then ask the man:

'Wilt thou have this woman to thy wedded wife, to live together according to God's law in the holy estate of matrimony? Wilt thou love her, comfort her, honour and keep her in sickness and in health; and forsaking all other, keep thee only unto her, so long as ye both shall live?'

ALTAR

CHOIR STALLS

CHOIR STALLS

MINISTER

BRIDE   GROOM

BRIDE'S FATHER

BEST MAN

CHIEF BRIDESMAID

PEWS

PEWS

BRIDE'S

BRIDEGROOM'S

BRIDESMAIDS

RELATIONS

RELATIONS

AND FRIENDS

AND FRIENDS

2. Positions during the service.

The man shall answer: 'I will.'

The clergyman then asks the woman:

> 'Wilt thou have this man to thy wedded husband, to live
> together according to God's law in the holy estate of
> matrimony? Wilt thou love him, comfort him, honour,
> and keep him in sickness and health; and forsaking all
> other, keep thee only to him, so long as ye both shall
> live?'

The woman shall answer: 'I will.'

The clergyman will then ask:

> 'Who giveth this woman to be married to this man?'

Immediately, the bride's father passes his daughter's right
hand to the clergyman, palm downwards. He passes it into
the hand of the bridegroom.

The bride's father's part in the service is now ended and he
may, if he wishes, drop back and take his place in the front
pew beside his wife, as unobtrusively as possible.

The bridegroom will then say after the clergyman:

> 'I ... take thee ... to my wedded wife, to have and to
> hold from this day forward, for better for worse, for
> richer for poorer, in sickness and in health, to love and
> to cherish, till death us do part, according to God's holy
> law; and thereto I give thee my troth.'

The pair will free their hands and then the bride will take
the right hand of the man in her own right hand and say after
the clergyman:

> 'I ... take thee ... to my wedded husband, to have and
> to hold from this day forward, for better for worse, for
> richer for poorer, in sickness and in health, to love and

to cherish, till death us do part, according to God's holy law; and thereto I give thee my troth.'

As they free their hands the best man takes the wedding ring from his waistcoat pocket and places it on the surface of the open prayer book proffered by the clergyman. After a prayer for the blessing of the ring, the clergyman will offer the ring to the bridegroom who will take it and place it on the third finger of the bride's left hand. (She should not be wearing her engagement ring or any other ring on that finger.)

While the bridegroom holds the ring in place, he must repeat after the clergyman:

'With this ring I thee wed, with my body I thee honour and all my worldly goods with thee I share: In the Name of the Father, and of the Son, and of the Holy Ghost. Amen.'

It is sometimes the case these days that the bride wishes to give a ring to the bridegroom. When this is so, the best man gives both rings to the clergyman and they are both blessed. The bride puts the ring on the bridegroom's finger after she herself has received the ring he is giving her, either silently or both say the words together.

These prayers are according to the Revised Service Series 1. Sometimes a couple chooses to be married with the words of the 1662 Prayer Book, which includes the promise by the bride to obey her husband.

Couples also have the choice of using a new wedding service from the Alternative Service Book 1980. The introduction is different, the giving away is optional, there are prayers for both bride and groom when giving the ring, and provision is made for a couple who are active members of the church to have the ceremony during a service of Holy Communion.

The clergyman may give a short address. A hymn may be sung instead of the psalm. The Alternative Service Book provides for prayers written or chosen by the couple in consultation with the clergyman.

This concludes the official ceremony and is followed by the nuptial blessing, prayers and a psalm.

As soon as it is over the clergyman or verger will lead the way to the vestry, or sometimes a chapel, followed in procession by the newly-married couple, the bridegroom's father with the bride's mother, the bride's father with the bridegroom's mother, the best man and the chief bridesmaid, the other bridesmaids and pages and perhaps one or two others.

In the vestry the bride signs the register – in her maiden name probably for the last time (though legally she may choose whether or not to take her husband's surname in the future), followed by her husband, the clergyman and two witnesses, for example the best man and the chief bridesmaid.

As soon as the registration is completed, the organist will get the signal and immediately the bridal couple will start the recessional. The bride will walk with her hand on her husband's left arm and with her veil thrown clear of her face.

The rest of the party will walk behind in the same order as they occupied before except that the bridesmaids will be immediately behind the couple and the best man will have slipped out to reach the church door in advance of the bridal party, if the church has a suitable unobtrusive exit.

There is likely to be considerable delay at this point. As well as the official photographer, because amateur photography has captured the interests of many, a number of friends of the bride and bridegroom will want to take the opportunity, if the weather is fine, to photograph the newlyweds, their bridesmaids, the official party – and indeed the church and the congregation, as it strolls out into the light of day.

As a sort of Master of Ceremonies, the best man needs to keep a check on the time. The whole party is due to arrive at the reception rooms at a pre-stated time – and if there is any unnecessary delay, the result might be a cold meal or a very short reception.

ALTAR

CHOIR STALLS

CHOIR STALLS

BRIDE'S FATHER

GROOM'S MOTHER

GROOM'S FATHER

BRIDE'S MOTHER

PEWS

PEWS

BRIDE'S

BRIDEGROOM'S

BRIDESMAIDS

RELATIONS

RELATIONS

AND FRIENDS

AND FRIENDS

GROOM   BRIDE

3. The recessional.

The best man makes sure that the bride and her husband enter their car first – followed in succession by their parents, bridesmaids, family and guests.

The best man has still one duty to perform at the church before he leaves; he may still have to settle the bridegroom's expenses in the form of marriage fees, organist's fees and any other out-of-pocket expenses that may have arisen on the spot.

All fees are usually settled well before the day, but, if not, the best man has this duty at the service. If there is no opportunity for him to have a word with the clergyman before or afterwards, there is no objection to the fees being placed in a sealed envelope and given to the verger to be delivered in due course. Fees are generally paid in one lump.

Confetti should not be strewn in the churchyard, simply because of good manners – never mind the laws regarding litter! It should be reserved for after the reception as the couple leave.

The best man will need to be at the reception fairly quickly, and if he is wise, he will either have one of the ushers standing by with a car, or arrange for a taxi to be available.

A few additional reminders might be of value at this point.

(a) During the recessional there is no reason why the bridal couple should not smile and nod to their friends as they walk slowly down the nave – but there must be no pause or conversation inside the church. During the processional before the service, the attention of the bride must not wander. Her gaze should be directed towards the clergyman or the altar, until she stands beside her bridegroom.

(b) Though it is usual for women to wear some form of head-dress in church, there is no obligation on them to do so. This freedom applies to the Church of England, the Roman Catholic church and some of the Free Churches. It does not apply in a Jewish synagogue, where all heads must be covered.

(c) The strewing of confetti about church premises, either

inside or outside, is frowned upon as untidy and creates unnecessary work for the verger.

(d) It has been known for the signing of the register to be delayed because of the lack of a pen or because, though a pen has been available, it has dried up!

(e) If for some particular reason, a clergyman other than the incumbent of the church where the wedding ceremony is to be held, is invited to conduct the service, it is usual to pay each of them the marriage fee. Such an invitation may be extended to a clergyman who happens to be a close relative or a particular friend of either the bride or the bridegroom.

(f) It is usually possible to have the church bells pealed for twenty minutes immediately prior to the ceremony and for up to half an hour afterwards where a church possesses them. There will, of course, be an extra charge for this and the organist should be consulted together with the verger.

(g) Many clergymen like to go through the service with each couple in church before the wedding day. The bridal gown is not needed for this purpose, though it is wise to provide some mock bouquets for the young bridesmaids so that they may become accustomed to carrying them when rehearsing their part. Similarly, if a train is to be worn by the bride, a few yards of almost any material will suffice for the rehearsal.

Both the clergyman and the verger should be consulted about the arrangements.

Though the ceremony is exactly the same where the bride happens to be a *widow*, tradition calls for less formality and suggests the omission of the bridal gown, and the veil. Similarly the bridegroom should wear a dark lounge suit rather than the formal attire usual at a bride's 'first' wedding.

Nor is the bride supported by bridesmaids, though a 'dame of honour' usually attends her. The dame of honour may be chosen by her from amongst sisters of her own or the bridegroom's, or a close friend.

If there is no procession before the service, the dame of

honour should wait for the bride at the chancel steps and her only duty is to relieve the bride of her bouquet.

Nor is there any obligation on anyone to 'give the bride away', though she may invite her father or some other male relative to do so.

The ceremony tends to be simple but the same restriction need not be placed on the reception afterwards – if there has been some lapse of time since the bride's first husband died.

In such case a wedding cake, floral decorations and speeches are quite permissible.

Other points include:

(a) The bridegroom should be attended by a best man. Ushers may be brought in, but as the ceremony is usually less ostentatious and less formal, there is rarely any need for them at a bride's 'second' marriage.

(b) Not later than the day before her 'second' wedding, the bride should remove her 'first' wedding ring – and never wear it again.

(c) If the wedding takes place within a year of the first husband's death, the service and the reception afterwards should be confined to members of the bride and bridegroom's family and only a very few friends.

The marriage of a *widower* is much less restricted by convention than in the case of a widow. However, it is commonly less formal than a first wedding – but the decision is that of the bride. Her wishes should be followed in the matter of the service, the formality, the number of guests and the scale of the reception afterwards.

The bride would be quite in order if she wore a bridal gown and a veil, was attended by bridesmaids and be 'given away' by her father.

Though the civil law permits the re-marriage of *divorced persons*, it is forbidden by the law of the Church of England. Nor may a clergyman be compelled to permit the re-marriage of a divorced person, by anyone else, in his church.

This means that no marriage service can be performed in a church of the Church of England where either the bride or the bridegroom have a previous partner still living, unless the clergyman is prepared to ignore the church authorities. But see page 84.

The marriage must therefore be a civil affair, generally speaking, conducted by a Superintendent Registrar in a register office.

Such a marriage is a simple affair lasting but a few minutes. No religious service is involved and all that is required is that the marriage vows are exchanged and the register signed; two witnesses being present and signing as such. This means a civil marriage in a register office can be as informal or as dressy as the parties concerned wish to make it.

Weddings can be conducted in full bridal regalia – the bride in a long white dress, attended by bridesmaids and pages, and the groom, best man and male guests in morning dress. Where the wedding room is large enough as many as 50–60 guests can be accommodated and there will be flower arrangements to complement the bridal party – in fact everything to make the ceremony as 'special' as possible. It has been known for brides to arrive at some register offices in horse drawn carriages or white Rolls Royces.

On the other hand, it can be a very simple and small affair, with informal dress, and perhaps just the two necessary witnesses accompanying the bride and groom.

Double Wedding: That is, the marriage of two couples before the same clergyman or Superintendent Registrar of Marriages, at the same time and in the same ceremony are by no means rare occurrences. Less common are ceremonies binding three separate couples in wedlock at the same time. Larger groups are not unknown and indeed there is nothing to prohibit a mass wedding, linking together any number of couples at the same service.

However, the cause for such massive ceremonies is rare in this country and multiple weddings are more often than not confined to family celebrations. Most common of all such occasions is the simultaneous marriage of sisters, or of twins, to their chosen partners.

A double wedding calls for precisely the same detailed prior arrangements as those applicable to anybody about to marry. Each one of them must give the same notice; each couple must be separately licenced and, of course, distinct certificates of marriages will be issued to each of the couples.

The brides will have their own bridesmaids and a best man will be chosen by each of the bridegrooms. The brides will walk down the aisle side-by-side to join their waiting bridegrooms. The two couples will then stand before the clergyman side-by-side, each bridegroom on the right of his bride.

The single ceremony will embrace both couples and only the responses will be made individually.

The recession must generally be made in separate parties because of the narrowness of the usual aisle, each party being complete in itself. The leading couple will assume that place by arrangement and not because of any 'right', though it is usual to allow the elder of the two men to escort his bride and their attendants from the church first.

13

THE CEREMONY BY OTHER RITES AND CIVIL MARRIAGES

The Roman Catholic Church

There are two differing types of service for those marrying within the rites of the Roman Catholic Church (whether or not both parties are Catholic).

The more usual rite consists of the offering of the Holy Mass during which the marriage vows are made and blessed, and a special blessing is given to the bridal couple.

The simpler ceremony consists of the taking and blessing of the marriage vows. It differs from the more elaborate rite only ceremonially – the vows are equally binding.

In the Roman Catholic Church a 'mixed marriage' is one between a Roman Catholic and someone who is not a baptized member of the Roman Catholic Church. It applies equally to a marriage between a Roman Catholic and someone baptized in some other faith, and between a Roman Catholic and somebody who is not baptized at all.

A 'Dispensation' will be required from the parish priest of the Catholic member of the bridal pair.

Two conditions are laid down for the granting of such a dispensation:

(a) The Catholic must promise to preserve his/her faith and to do his/her best to ensure that any children of the marriage will be baptized and brought up in the Catholic faith.

(b) The clergyman must be able to sign a statement saying that in his opinion the non-Catholic will not oppose the fulfilment of the promise made by the Catholic.

It is increasingly common for all couples who are marrying in the Catholic Church to be asked to attend some form of 'preparation'. This is wider than 'religious instruction', and covers a number of points which are common to all marriages as well as those in which a Roman Catholic is involved. The purpose of this is to try to ensure that the couple are adequately prepared for marriage and have a reasonable understanding of what they are doing.

Such a marriage will normally take place in the Catholic church; but for good reasons a dispensation can be granted even from this.

In both forms of marriage the bride is conducted by her father to the bridegroom standing before the altar. At the appropriate moment in the ceremony the father of the bride 'gives her away' by placing her right hand in the right hand of the bridegroom.

After the exchange of vows there follows the blessing of the ring(s). The husband places the ring on his wife's finger with the words: '... (Christian name only), take this ring as a sign of my love and fidelity. In the name of the Father and of the Son, and of the Holy Spirit.'

If there are two rings, the wife places a ring on her husband's finger saying the same words. At the end of the ceremony the bridal couple sign the register accompanied by at least two witnesses.

When the marriage ceremony takes place during Mass it is customary for the Catholics who are present to receive Holy Communion in the service. The bride and bridegroom will also be invited to choose the readings beforehand and to read out the passages from the scripture themselves during the Mass. If they prefer, however, the clergyman will do the readings or invite someone else to do so. This part of the service is where you can bring your own personal 'touch' to the proceedings, by choosing a piece from the scriptures which has, perhaps, special meanings for you and your loved one. Naturally, if a passage is chosen which is more relevant to the wedding service, so much the better, and this can make the whole proceedings fuller and richer.

Chief Bridesmaid, Bridesmaids and Best Man

The chief bridesmaid stations herself on the bride's left at the altar after attending to the bride's wedding veil, and after taking charge of the bridal bouquet. The best man stands to the right of the bridegroom – and the bridesmaids form into a line behind, facing the altar.

When the Mass is ended, the protocol afterwards, when the bride and bridegroom leave the Sanctuary, is for the bridesmaids and the best man to take their places again; the chief bridesmaid on the right arm of the best man; they follow the bridal couple. Behind them all follow the bridesmaids in pairs – and the procession then moves in the recessional down the aisle to the church door. Now is the time for the photographers to move in and snap the group, including the wedding guests who have now left the church door.

Afterwards, the whole party proceed to the scene of the wedding reception.

A few points to be remembered include:

(a) The bride signs the register in her maiden name – for the last time.

(b) The witnesses who are to sign the register should be chosen well in advance. This prevents any confusion arising after the service is completed, and the chosen group proceed to the Sanctuary. The usual persons chosen to accompany the bridal pair as witnesses of the signatures are the best man and the chief bridesmaid, but in any event, each person who is a witness should be 18 years of age or over. Bear this in mind if you have chosen a particularly young chief bridesmaid or best man.

(c) The re-marriage of divorced persons is strictly refused

in the Catholic Church. However, there may often be cases where the previous marriage, for some reason, is not recognised by the Church; perhaps because it did not comply with church law as in the case of those who were originally married in a civil register office, and not in a church. In this case, a church marriage would normally be permitted.

(d) In any event it is essential to consult the clergyman who is to conduct your service at least six months in advance. This is for your own benefit as if there are any 'snags' to be ironed out, you will have plenty of time to get them organised, and the clergyman will have time to adequately prepare both parties before marrying them in his church.

The Free Churches

In the majority of Free Church denominations the church itself will have been registered by a Superintendent Registrar of Marriages as a building in which marriages may be solemnized. Ministers of the United Reformed Church, the Baptist, Methodist and other Protestant churches have long taken advantage of their rights, under the Marriage Act of 1898, to become registered as 'authorised' persons; that is, to have applied for and received sanction both to conduct the service and to act as the registrar under the civil law.

Others, for various reasons, have not sought such authority and in consequence though they may conduct a marriage ceremony, a Superintendent Registrar, or his deputy, must be present to record the wedding, or a separate civil ceremony must be conducted by a Superintendent Registrar in his office.

Wherever the venue of a marriage, the register must be signed by the bridal couple after they have made their vows and the fact must be witnessed by the signatures of two onlookers.

In all cases, the order of service is a matter left almost entirely to the religious scruples of the couple who are to be married, and, of course, to the special rites of the church whose blessing they seek.

Certain requirements must be met in the solemnization of all Free Church weddings. They are:

(a) Both the bride and the bridegroom must be at least 18 years of age or have the written consent of their parents.

(b) They must be unmarried or legally divorced.

(c) Proper notice must have been given of the intention to marry in accordance with the civil law.

(d) The service must take place in a registered building.

(e) The minister must be an authorised person, or a Superintendent Registrar, or his deputy, must be present, or else a separate service must be conducted in the Superintendent Registrar's office.

(f) At some point in the service the following declarations must be made in the presence of the minister, if he is an authorised person – or before a Registrar:

(i) 'I do solemnly declare that I know not of any lawful impediment why I ... may not be joined in matrimony to ...'

(ii) To each other in turn, 'I call upon these persons here present to witness that I ... do take thee ... to my lawful wedded husband (or wife, as the case may be).'

(g) Each must sign the marriage register as should two witnesses of the marriage in proof thereof.

The variety of detail in the ceremonies of the different denominations is considerable – sometimes merely a matter of detail, sometimes they are fundamental.

In almost every case, however, the order of service follows, roughly, that customary in the Church of England, some of the details of which include:

1. The procession.

2. The bride stands before the minister to the left of her bridegroom, during the service. Her father, or whoever is to give her away, on her left. The best man stands on the right of the bridegroom.

3. The service begins with the declaration of intent.

4. The minister will call upon the congregation to voice any legal objection to the marriage.

5. The couple exchange vows as required by law and then give and receive a ring or rings.

6. Receive the blessing of the church.

7. Sign the register.

In all cases the minister concerned should be consulted well in advance of the projected date of the wedding. Some churches are more ornate in their ceremonial than others, some more formal and yet others are extremely simple.

Although it is general for the Free Churches to view a marriage as binding for life, it is usually within the discretion of each minister to consider the re-marriage of a divorced person, considering each individual case in the light of its own merits.

Some ministers may be found to be adamant in their refusal to marry a person who has been divorced, others will take cognisance of who was the injured party and yet others may consider the whole circumstances – even to the point of charity. Obviously the most careful enquiries need to be made by the couple concerned, before completing any arrangements, in such an event.

The Quakers (Religious Society of Friends)

A Quaker marriage is very different from most other wedding services. It is extremely simple and altogether free of ceremonial.

The first step to such a marriage needs to be taken at least six weeks in advance of the proposed date and the procedure is as follows:

(a) Application should be made to the registering officer of the monthly meeting within the bounds of which it is desired that the marriage should take place.

(b) For each non-Quaker applicant, support in writing must be obtained from two adult members of the Society, given on forms which the registering officer will supply; if the registering officer assents to the application he will supply the party or parties with the appropriate form for the Superintendent Registrar.

(c) The couple must then make application to marry in accordance with civil law through the Superintendent Registrar of Marriages in the district in which they live – or if they live in different districts, notice must be given to the Registrar in each.

(d) Notice of the intended marriage is given by the Quaker registering officer at the Sunday morning meeting or meetings to which the parties belong or which they usually attend or in the area in which they live. If no written objection is received, the registering officer will ask the appropriate meeting to appoint a meeting for worship for the solemnization of the marriage.

(e) Public notice of such a meeting will be given at the place at which it is to be held at the close of the previous meeting for worship.

The service, as any Quaker meeting, is held on the basis of silent communion of the spirit: there is neither pageantry nor music, set service nor sermon; there is, however, opportunity for those who may feel moved by the spirit to give a spoken message or prayer.

There is not necessarily a bridesmaid or a best man; a morning coat is unusual and the bride's dress will be fairly simple; there is neither a procession nor a recessional afterwards.

But at some point during the meeting the bride and groom will rise and hand-in-hand make their declaration of marriage.

The bridegroom will say:

'Friends, I take this my friend ... to be my wife, promising through divine assistance, to be unto her a loving and faithful husband, so long as we both on earth shall live.'

The bride makes a similar declaration. The wedding certificate is then signed by the bridal couple and by two of the witnesses. The certificate is read aloud by the registering officer and after the meeting it is usual for all others present to add their names to it.

The wedding ring plays no official part in the marriage, though it is common for the couple either to exchange rings afterwards, or for the groom to give one to his bride.

It is usual at the close of the meeting for worship for the couple to withdraw with four witnesses and the registering officer to complete the civil marriage register.

The Society retains its belief in the sanctity and life-long nature of marriage, but recognises that it may in certain circumstances be right to make a new start, and the re-marriage of a divorced person may be allowed at the discretion of the monthly meeting.

The Jewish Wedding

Synagogue marriage in Britain is both a civil and religious ceremony. The requirements of both must be satisfied before the marriage can take place. Two separate applications for permission to marry are necessary.

Each party makes a personal visit, about eight weeks before the wedding, to the register office of their home district. After 21 days the Superintendent Registrar issues his Certificate of Marriage. This must be sent or brought to the Synagogue. Marriage at short notice can be arranged by a special licence obtainable from the Registrar for an additional fee.

The parties must attend the Office of the Chief Rabbi, Alder House, Tavistock Square, London, WC1, or the Religious Authority under which their ceremony is taking place as early as possible, and not later than three weeks before the wedding, to apply for the Chief Rabbi's authorisation. Outside London, your local Minister or Secretary for Marriages can arrange this.

Normally on the Sabbath prior to the wedding, the bridegroom is called up to the Reading of the Law in Synagogue.

It is customary for bride and groom to fast on the wedding day until after the ceremony.

Etiquette at the Synagogue can vary. However, the groom is always expected to arrive first. Usually he sits in the Warden's box with his father, future father-in-law, and best man.

The groom takes his place first under the *chuppah* (wedding canopy), the best man stands behind and to his left with the ring handy.

The bride is generally brought in by her father, followed by bridesmaids, bride's mother with escort (or male relative), and bridegroom's parents. According to old Jewish custom, however, the bride is brought in by her mother and future mother-in-law. Both sets of parents usually stand beneath the *chuppah*.

Before the bride comes under the *chuppah* the groom is formally requested by the Minister to approve the appointment of two witnesses of the *ketubah* (marriage document) and accept the terms and conditions of the *ketubah* whereby he undertakes a number of obligations to his wife.

The bride stands under the *chuppah* at the groom's right. At each side of the *chuppah* stand the *unterfuhrers*, usually the couple's parents.

Next come the blessings of betrothal, recited over a cup of wine. The first blessing is for wine and the second praises God for commanding us concerning forbidden marriages.

In Jewish law, the couple become married when the man places the ring on the woman's finger, with her acceptance signifying consent. It is important to note that this act effecting their union is carried out by the parties themselves; it is not the Minister who 'marries' them, but they who marry each other, and the Minister's presence is as a Jewish law expert, and sometimes as witness to the *ketubah* as well as in a civil capacity if he is Secretary for Marriages.

Since the ring has such importance, it must be the groom's property; should be of precious metal, but without jewels, and the bride should wear no other rings or jewellery during the ceremony. The ring is placed on the bride's right index finger, but she may transfer it to the 'ring finger' later. The reason for Jewish insistence on a plain ring is to allow no difference between rich and poor and to avoid any deception or misunderstanding as to its value. It is placed on the right index finger because in ancient transactions this finger was used symbolically to acquire things.

The groom recites in Hebrew a declaration:

'Behold, thou art consecrated unto me by this ring according to the law of Moses and of Israel'.

implying that the requirements of Jewish law have been met.

The *ketubah* is now read in Aramaic original and in English abstract and handed to the bride. She should look after it carefully since it is her interests which it recognises, and should it be lost she should get it replaced.

Then follow the seven blessings of marriage, with the final words of prayer that the bride and groom might find the perfect happiness of Adam and Eve and live a life of 'joy and gladness, mirth and exultation, pleasure and delight, love and brotherhood, peace and companionship'. At the conclusion of the betrothal and the marriage blessings, the couple sip wine to symbolise the fact that they must share the same cup of life whether it be sweet or otherwise. This is followed by the breaking of a glass by the groom.

The ceremony concludes by the Minister pronouncing the blessing, in the heartfelt wish that its words of blessing, protection, grace and peace be fulfilled for bride and groom.

The couple sign the marriage documents, the bride signing her maiden name. The group leave the Synagogue in procession with their attendants. Before greeting their guests at the reception they should spend a few moments together in private (*yihud*) denoting their newly-acquired status as husband and wife entitled to live together under the same roof.

Civil Marriages

Often, for various reasons, a couple may prefer to marry free of any religious obligations. It may be that they have different, irreconcilable, religious beliefs, maybe divorce has cut one or both of them off from their church, or possibly, family objections have decided them to marry privately and without more than the minimum of ceremony necessary to make public and legal their new status.

Under a certificate of marriage obtainable from a Superintendent Registrar anyone legally entitled to marry, must be married by him not less than 21 days after due notice has been given and published. Where the couple apply for a licence and satisfy the legal requirements for the issue of such a document – as detailed in Chapter 4, the ceremony may be performed by the Superintendent Registrar after the expiration of one clear working day, except a Sunday, Good Friday, or Christmas Day, from the date of the entry of the notice.

Such a marriage entails no religious service; all that is expected is that the following vows will be exchanged before a Superintendent Registrar and two witnesses:

'I do solemnly declare that I know not of any lawful impediment why I ... may not be joined in matrimony to ...' and to one another in turn: 'I call upon these persons here present to witness that I ... do take thee ... to be my lawful wedded husband (or 'wife').'

Then follows the signing of the marriage register by each

of the newlyweds and those witnessing the event.

The symbol of the wedding ring from the bridegroom to the bride is common practice, but has no legal significance under civil law.

A Superintendent Registrar has no legal right to refuse to re-marry a divorced person. The civil law takes no cognisance of religious beliefs or scruples in such cases and so long as the decree absolute has been granted and all other legal requirements have been met, the Superintendent Registrar is duty bound to perform the marriage ceremony.

14

CELEBRATIONS

After the wedding ceremony comes the reception and this can be as formal or informal as you wish to make it. The main criteria will be how much money is to be spent and how many guests have to be invited. This will help you to decide whether you hold the reception in the bride's home, quite often with a marquee to give added space, in a village or church hall where there are usually tables, chairs, cloak-rooms and kitchen facilities already, or in a restaurant or hotel which provide all the necessary services including a room for the bride to change in.

The modern house is generally too small in which to entertain more than a limited number of guests, and rarely big enough to accommodate all those who expect and feel entitled to be invited.

This can be overcome by hiring a marquee or lean-to awning to extend the space available and these normally come in widths of 20, 30 and 40 feet and in any length. Many firms provide coloured roof and wall linings complete with chandeliers, wall bracket lights or spot lights, and both matting and wooden flooring are available. Such firms will also provide chairs and tables and a range of heaters should the wedding be during the cold months.

If the bride's mother is a good and highly organised cook it is quite possible for her to prepare and freeze food beforehand and she will need to choose items that can be served easily so that she is not trying to be cook, waitress and hostess on the day. She will also have to hire or borrow enough chairs and small tables, china and cutlery and get the local off-licence to provide a wine waiter or two in addition to supplying the wine and the glasses. Alternatively, a firm of caterers can be brought in who will suggest suitable menus, provide the linen, china and silver as well as serving the food and clearing up afterwards. Most caterers will also serve and deal with the drinks even if they have not provided the wine or the glasses. The bride's mother will also have to organise the flowers and table decorations.

It is becoming increasingly common for families who have hired a marquee to hold a reception followed by a disco in the evening.

If the house is large enough a room should be set aside for the display of wedding presents as this gives guests the opportunity to inspect the presents and for the two families to get to know one another better.

The hall will be needed as a reception room where the host and hostess can receive and welcome their guests. The bride's brothers and sisters, the bridesmaids and the best man should be briefed to keep the flow of guests passing beyond the reception point towards the main rooms without pause. As they arrive the guests should shake hands with the bride's mother first and then her father. Immediately afterwards they meet the bridegroom's parents followed by the bride and bridegroom in that order. To prevent any hold-ups everyone should make their greetings brief and save longer conversations until after all the guests have been received.

At large weddings this can take a long time so sometimes the reception line is dispensed with, and the guests are received briefly by bride and groom only.

At this point the guests will be offered a drink – sherry, still or sparkling white wine, with apple, grape or orange juice for those who want it, and they will circulate until the bride and bridegroom make a move towards the buffet table, or if it is to be a sit down meal, to their places at the top table. When the bride and groom have been served or served themselves from the table, it is the general signal for everyone else to do so and they can then either circulate with their food, or take it to a table and join other guests in an informal way.

Where a luncheon or other meal is to be served, the bride and bridegroom sit at the head of the table, the bride on her husband's left. The bride's mother sits next to the bridegroom and the bridegroom's mother on the left of the

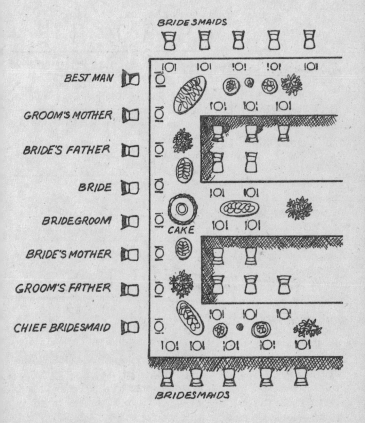

4. The top table.

bride's father who sits next to his newly-married daughter. The best man and the chief bridesmaid make up the top table as shown in Fig. 4. Alternatively, the best man and chief bridesmaid can take places beside the bride and groom, with the parents further out from the centre, in which case the table would look like Fig. 5. If the groom's parents and

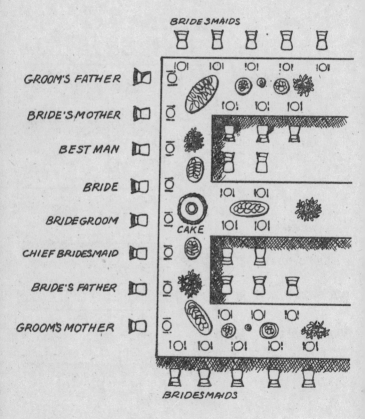

5. Alternative top table.

bride's parents prefer to sit each beside their own partners, then this can be accommodated with the layout in Fig. 6.

Depending on the space available, the caterer will suggest how the tables and chairs can best be placed so that all those who wish to sit down can do so. Where there is to be a 'serve yourself' buffet, the cake and the bride's bouquet are put at

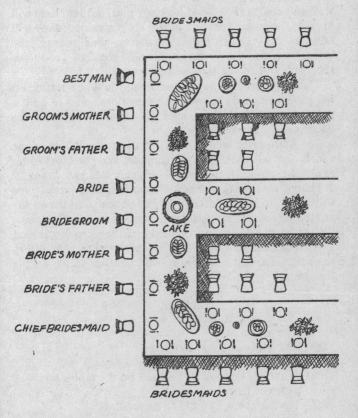

6. Another alternative.

one end, and the bride and groom will stand to one side of the cake during the speeches and toasts.

If the reception is held in a village hall, town hall or other rooms, an area needs to be kept clear in which the guests are greeted and here again a caterer will be able to suggest the best way of arranging the room or rooms.

Most medium and large hotels have the facilities and often specialise in the organisation of wedding receptions. Their staff will cook and serve almost any meal desired; they will provide the wines and give advice on the subject; they will arrange the tables, the decorations, cloakrooms, the reception room, the dining room, and if required a room for the display of the newly-wed's presents.

Their commissionaire, or doorman, should be outside on the pavement ready to open the car doors – and to keep a space free of parked vehicles immediately opposite the entrance.

The hall porter will be ready to direct the guests to the apartments allocated for the function and the cloakroom attendants ready to receive the cloaks, coats and wraps.

Sherry, white wine and non-alcoholic apple or grape juice will be poured into glasses ready to be served as the guests arrive and the waitresses briefed to move among them with their trays all prepared and loaded with the reception drinks.

Arrangements for all receptions need to be made well in advance. The host and hostess will have to decide on the following:

(a) The time and date.
(b) The menu.
(c) The wines and soft drinks.
(d) Who is to make and ice the cake.
(e) What flowers are to be used on the tables and who provides them?
(f) The number of guests to be present.
(g) The bride's changing room.
(h) The seating plan if one is needed.

A reception after the wedding ceremony is intended to allow the wedding guests to congratulate the newly-weds, to join in the toasts to the health and happiness of the couple, to witness the cutting of the cake and to wish them well as they leave for their honeymoon. It is also an opportunity for the two families to get to know each other better.

The meal itself is incidental to the celebrations and is served because the guests will be hungry long before the bride and bridegroom leave for their honeymoon – especially if they travelled any distance to attend the wedding. As the meal has always been an essential need, it has long been the custom to use it for the high-spot feature of the celebrations. During it, the toasts are given, the cake cut and the greetings messages read to the guests.

Because of this, all the arrangements need a great deal of thought and careful planning.

There are many methods and fashions in which to conduct a ceremonial wedding breakfast – or lunch – or tea – or evening reception or disco. Few of the arrangements are obligatory, though custom lays down certain broad highlights. The main thing to remember is that it is the day of the newly-weds.

ADVANCE ARRANGEMENTS

The wedding cake. The cake must be ordered many weeks in advance of the wedding and apart from the style and decorations, its size should be considered in relation to the number of guests expected to attend the reception and those who will expect to receive a portion who were unable to be present. It is quite common for the cake to be home-made and professionally iced. It should be delivered in good time to the caterer at the reception rooms – either the night before or early on the wedding day.

The flowers. The caterer will be glad to receive the flowers that have been ordered by the bride's mother for the tables as early as possible on the morning of the reception. Besides flowers for the tables one or two large arrangements may be necessary and a florist will always provide these if the family have no good 'flower arranging' friends. If a posy is required for the top of the wedding cake this can also be provided by the florist.

Menus and other printed material. Details of the menu and wines will have been settled weeks in advance of the wedding date between the bride's parents and the caterer or hotelier. If menus are required these should be ordered and printed then, along with paper serviettes with the names or initials of the bride and bridegroom, place cards, drink mats, ash trays and book matches. Samples of these items can be seen at any large stationers (W.H. Smith for example) and can be ordered through them to meet your own requirements.

Whatever is ordered should be in the hands of the caterer the day before the wedding – not forgetting the need to write the guests' names on the place cards.

The reception rooms. Although the rooms required for the reception will have been agreed with the caterer and booked some time in advance there are still a few arrangements which must be completed by the host. If they have hired a hall, it is as well to check with the caretaker that the hall will have been cleaned the day before, that there are adequate tables and chairs, whether or not the hall provides towels and soap in the cloakrooms, to check that there are enough hangers for coats in the cloakrooms and whether the hall has its own flower vases for large arrangements.

If the wedding presents are to be exhibited the caterer will need to know how many trestle tables will be required and if a separate room is used it should be cleared of unnecessary furniture. On the afternoon before the wedding the bride's parents, the bride and bridegroom and possibly the best man will make a display of the gifts (making sure to keep the wrappings and boxes so that they can be transported safely after the wedding reception). Each gift should have a small card with the name of the giver on it. Cheques should be listed on a card with no mention of the amount given.

If the presents are valuable, they should be insured to include their display. Though a hotelier will do his best to safeguard them overnight and during the reception, he is unlikely to accept responsibility for theft or damage. The room would be locked overnight and unlocked as the guests are due to arrive. It is up to the bridal party to remove the presents afterwards.

The seating arrangements for a 'sit down' meal.

The caterer will need to have a general idea of how many guests are to be entertained some time in advance of the event – and he should be given final details, together with the seating plan and the place-cards not later than the evening before the wedding.

There are certain formalities concerning the seating arrangements – though a hostess should not distress herself if she finds it more convenient, or a happier solution, to seat people in some other manner.

This plan cannot be made without the assistance of the caterer who will advise on the layout of the tables to suit the numbers involved, the shape and style of the room and the service points.

The top table is the most important and the main preoccupation of the planner and the simplest arrangements are those already given on page 115.

So far as other guests are concerned, brothers and sisters should be interspersed by their wives and husbands – where applicable. Uncles and aunts follow and then the friends of the newly-weds.

The length of the side tables will depend largely on the size and shape of the room and the number of guests to be seated.

If there is plenty of room only the outer sides may be used

so that everybody has a clear view of everybody else.

Usually this is impracticable – or it would make the tables stretch out to such a length that those towards the foot of each arm will be out of touch with the top table. In such case the inner sides of the arms should be used.

In no circumstances should the inner side of the top table be used for seating purposes. The cake, on a small separate table in front of the bridal couple, should be the only thing to screen their faces.

Of course even larger layouts may be used.

And for numbers in excess of, perhaps, 200, an attractive arrangement can be made with separate tables set at an angle to the top table, so that not one of the guests will have their backs fully turned towards the newly-weds:

This plan can be extended to suit the room, either by adding extra sprigs if the room is long, or by lengthening them if it is broad.

However, your caterer will have expert knowledge and his advice must be sought.

After due consideration has been given to the arrangement for seating the members of the two families, their husbands and wives, and the friends of the bride and bridegroom, an attempt should be made to alternate the sexes as far as possible. And a good hostess will give thought to the problem of family feuds, jealousies and friendships.

Such likes and dislikes, if they are not sorted out before the reception, may well lead to quarrels, unhappy silences and outspoken comments. To separate antipathetic guests irrespective of their seating 'rights' is much better than to leave matters to take their course and hope for the best. This is the newly-weds 'day' and every effort must be made to keep it free of friction.

'Off-beat' guests might well be kept at a distance from the top table, humorists kept apart and younger couples with a personal interest in one another, placed happily side-by-side.

The suggestion is that the bride's family and friends should occupy the tables on the bridegroom's side of the room – and vice versa, but others will persuade the host and hostess that the families should be mixed as freely as possible. Both arrangements have a lot to commend them to the hostess. Mixing the families does tend to give them an opportunity to get to know one another, while segregation means less embarrassment to all concerned.

The table plan, with place marked with the name of a guest, should be given to the caterer to post up in a convenient place so that the guests will be able to go straight to their places as they enter the dining room – and confirm the actual seat by means of the place-card bearing his or her name, lying on the table by the plate.

THE ARRIVAL

Though the newly-weds leave the church first, it is important that the bride's parents arrive first at the reception. As host and hostess they must be the first to greet their guests as they arrive, if there is to be a reception line.

The reception line should consist of:

The bride's mother
The bride's father
The bridegroom's mother
The bridegroom's father
The bride
The bridegroom

in that order.

If the reception is to include a buffet meal, the reception by both sets of parents and the newly-weds almost invariably takes place immediately on the arrival of the guests, but if there is to be a luncheon, it is quite usual for the actual reception of the guests to take place later, as they pass into the dining room.

This is often preferred as it relieves the parents and the newly-weds of the duty to rush to the reception rooms from the church; gives the bride time to recover her composure;

enables the photographer to take his pictures of the cutting of the cake while the guests remove their coats and prepare themselves to meet other guests before passing along the reception line.

Assume that the reception is to take place immediately on the arrival of the guests. In this case, guests are greeted by their hosts and the bridal couple as they arrive – without regard to family seniority. The greetings must be brief if there is not to be a long line of impatiently waiting guests and the best man and bridesmaids should do their best to move them on by directing them towards the already poured drinks.

They should be encouraged, too, to circulate about the room, to meet one another – and, of course, take the opportunity to inspect the wedding presents.

The guests should arrive as promptly as possible so that the bridal party can finish with the greetings and then lead the guests towards the meal.

THE WEDDING MEAL

As soon as the last of the guests have been received the best man should lead the couple and other members of the bridal party to where their guests are conversing and enjoying a drink. They may join them for a while but must avoid standing in cliques or of allowing anyone to monopolise their attention.

They may spend a few minutes inspecting their wedding presents and discussing them with their guests – but the best man must keep his eye on the time.

As soon as the caterer or one of his staff indicates that the meal is ready, he should persuade the newly-weds to move towards the tables arm-in-arm.

Behind the newly-weds, the bridal party should be in the following order:

The bride's father with the bridegroom's mother.

The bridegroom's father with the bride's mother.
The best man with the chief bridesmaid.
The bridesmaids.
The pages – and the guests.

Before entering the dining room the guests should have examined the seating plan and so, with the help of the place-cards, should have little difficulty in locating their seats.

When everybody has found his or her place, the best man should obtain silence and if 'grace' is to be said, call upon the clergyman or minister present to 'say grace'. Often, in the absence of a clergyman or minister, a known member of a church among the guests may be invited to 'say grace'. But he or she should be approached in advance. Failing any of these arrangements the duty should be undertaken by the bride's father. One of the following forms of words would be suitable:

(a) *For our families, our friends and for this food which you give us, we thank you Lord.*
(b) *Receive our thanks, O Lord, for this food and for this happy day.*
(c) *We thank you, our Father, for good food which brings health, and human love which brings happiness.*
(d) *For what we are about to receive, may the Lord make us truly thankful and ever mindful of the needs of others.*

Grace is often neglected nowadays, but should never be omitted if a minister of religion is present.

THE SPEECHES

As soon as the guests appear to have reached the end of their meal, the toasts are drunk. The best man acts as toastmaster and it is he who calls on the first speaker when he thinks the time is ripe. This is either a close personal friend or relative of the bride – often her father. The toast is: 'The Health and Happiness of the Bride and Bridegroom'.

Though it is usual for this toast to be given by the bride's father – or guardian – it is not uncommon for that duty to be passed to some other male member of the bride's family who is deemed to be perhaps a better speaker or is someone of note. But the bride's father must remember to delegate such a task some days in advance and not have it sprung on some unsuspecting guest at the last moment.

The speech is usually of a semi-serious nature, especially if it is made by the father and generally includes:

1. The happiness he and his wife have experienced in the bringing up of their daughter, the treasure she has been to them and the loss they will feel following her marriage and move to a home of her own.

2. A couple of interludes in her life – one perhaps amusing, the other more serious.

3. A welcome into the family of the new son-in-law and the hope that it will be gaining a son rather than losing a daughter.

4. A welcome, too, to the bridegroom's parents.

5. Perhaps an episode concerning the bride and the bridegroom together – particularly if they have known one another for a number of years.

6. A little timely advice to the newly-weds, usually bound up with his own experiences in company with his wife – the bride's mother.

7. The toast of the Health and Happiness of the couple.

Of course this is merely a suggestion and it is probable that the proposer will have other things to say and other points to make. But he must make his speech with one eye on the clock – and the faces of his guests. The newly-weds may have a plane to catch – and the guests are easily bored by a lengthy speech.

The bridegroom then replies on behalf of his wife and himself, thanking the gathering for their good wishes and gifts; their parents for being their parents and all those who have helped to make the wedding ceremony and the reception a success – concluding with the bridesmaids, and in so doing proposes a toast to 'The bridesmaids'.

In the first part, responding to the toast proposed by the bride's father, or whoever has made it, the bridegroom might refer to:

1. The kindness of his parents during his boyhood, their care and attention to his upbringing.

2. The thanks he owes them for his start in life – and for any particular sacrifices they have made on his behalf.

3. A tribute to his wife's parents and anything they may have provided for the couple's future.

4. Perhaps a short episode of his meeting with his bride, of their engagement, difficulties or fortunes.

5. His intention to devote himself to the happiness of his bride.

And at this point the bridegroom may turn his attention to lighter matters and his toast to the bridesmaids, with perhaps:

6. Thanks to his best man for his assistance and possible nuisance value.

7. A reference to the beauty of the bridesmaids and his thanks for their help during the service.

At this point, if he has some small present for each of the young ladies, he will call them forward one after another to receive his gift.

Such presents are by no means mandatory and where given they usually comprise some small piece of jewellery. See page 82.

The best man then responds on behalf of the young ladies. His speech should be light and as far as possible filled with humour. From this point there should be no return to emotional references or serious topics – and the ability to make such a speech is often taken very much into consideration by the bridegroom when choosing his best man. He might refer to:

1. The bridegroom's luck in getting the bride he has – and how many another man has wept over her poor choice.

2. The difficulty in getting a scared bridegroom to the altar.

3. The joy he and his friends feel at getting rid of him from their bachelor ranks and their pity for an unfortunate bride.

4. And, of course, the thanks of the bridesmaids for the presents and good wishes they have received from the bridegroom.

Those three speeches compose the traditional toasts and replies customary in a wedding reception. No further speeches need be given and as often as not, they are considered sufficient – but it is by no means uncommon, where time permits, for other guests to speak. One most frequently favoured is a speech of thanks to the host and hostess, given usually by some relative of the bridegroom's – followed by a reply from the bride's father, very briefly if he has already spoken.

Other speeches are permissible, though the greatest need is to avoid boredom – particularly by insincere guests who like the sound of their own voices or who cannot bear not to have taken some noteworthy part in the proceedings.

With one eye on the time, the best man brings the speeches to an end by rising to read the messages of congratulations and good wishes that have arrived for the newly-weds. In reading them he should endeavour to introduce a few light, background comments on the contents and about those who have sent them. The reading of a large number of telemessages can soon become boring as they are usually repetitions and many of the names will be known to few of the guests.

The best man should remember to hand the telemessages to the bride's mother immediately after the reception to be kept until the bride's return from her honeymoon. It is her duty to write and acknowledge them as soon as possible afterwards – generally at the same time as she writes her thanks to those who have sent presents.

THE CAKE

The ceremony of cutting the cake follows. The bride should place the point of the knife near the centre of the bottom tier of the cake. The bridegroom places a hand over his wife's and slowly and carefully helps her to force the point of the blade down into the heart of the cake and then to draw the blade forward and downwards. They may cut a complete slice and share it between them, but due to the elaborate decorations on many cakes, the inexperience of the couple and the probable nervousness of the bride, they rarely make more than a token cut.

Usually that completes the formal 'cutting' of the cake. The caterer takes over from that point and after dismantling the tiers and ornaments, uses his experience to divide up a portion of the cake into handy, not over-large portions which the bridesmaids can help to distribute amongst the guests. If there is a large number of guests, the catering staff will do the distribution.

The remainder of the cake will then be set aside for eventual distribution to friends and relatives of the newly-weds who have been unable to attend the wedding and the reception afterwards.

It is traditional for the bridesmaids to keep their slices of cake and to place them under their pillows that night – in the belief that they will then dream of their own future husbands.

THE DEPARTURE

The bride then retires, to change from her wedding finery into her going-away clothes.

As she mounts the stairs to the room set aside for this purpose, it is traditional for the bridesmaids to gather at the foot or below the banisters – while the rest of the wedding party stands by to watch the fun.

From a convenient place on the stairs, the bride throws her bouquet to the young ladies gathered below – and the bridesmaid who captures the bouquet can, reputedly, expect to be the next bride. Or she throws her bouquet as she gets into the car to drive away, in a shower of confetti.

While she changes, her baggage is put with the bridegroom's at the exit, all ready to load into the car or taxi that is to take the pair of them on the first stage of the honeymoon.

The bridegroom, if he lives near the venue of the reception (or if one of his friends lives nearby) hurries off with his best man to change into his own going-away clothes. If this is not possible, the bridegroom usually finds a convenient spot among the reception rooms – and as his own dressing should take very much less time than that of his wife, he should be all ready and waiting when she comes down the stairs.

While he is waiting, the bridegroom collects from his best man the rail or air tickets and any other travel documents that he needs for the honeymoon.

When the bride is ready no further time should be wasted in which emotional scenes may arise. In the years long gone by partings of this nature were a much more final farewell than they are today. A bride's departure with her husband might mean a separation for years between her and her parents – sometimes, if they were going abroad, perhaps for ever. Tears and sorrow were natural under such circumstances – but modern travel has put the distant parts of the world within a few short hours of home, and with our present standards of living, it is not likely to be impossible for a young couple to save enough for a visit to their parents once in a while.

The occasion should therefore be joyful and a mother's inevitable tears kept from sight.

The farewells should be brisk, cheery and smiling. A new

and growing custom is for the groom to present his mother and mother-in-law with bouquets of flowers as they say goodbye.

Only after the newly-weds have finally departed for their honeymoon should the guests begin to leave – saying their final goodbyes to the host and hostess – the bride's mother and father – until only they and the best man remain behind to clear up the paraphernalia of presents, clothes, wedding cake – and the odds and ends that will surely be forgotten by their owners.

15

AFTER THE SHOW

Before leaving the reception rooms the bride's mother should remember to pick up what is left of the wedding cake. Almost certainly the caterer will have packed it in a box strong enough to protect what is left of the sugary confection.

She must gather up, pack and take away with her the wedding clothes left behind by her daughter – and make certain that none of her lady guests has left anything behind.

At the same time the best man will pack and take away the discarded clothes of the bridegroom – and see to it that nothing has been left behind by any of the male guests. He will hand over the greetings messages, if he has not already given them to the bride, to the bride's mother.

The best man may return later that day – together with the newly-weds' brothers and male friends, armed with boxes, packing cases, paper and string to gather up the collection of wedding presents from the room where they have been exhibited. They are then taken to the home of the bride's parents where they should be put on show in some little used room until such time as they are to be taken to the newly-weds' own home.

The best man will need to return the bridegroom's and his own wedding outfit if they have been hired. To purchase such clothing is unnecessary unless it is likely to be used regularly and nowadays it is usually hired.

The bride's mother will settle down to the task of dividing up sufficient of the wedding cake to be able to send a piece to the friends and relatives of the bride and bridegroom who were unable to attend the wedding and the reception afterwards – perhaps because of age, infirmity, illness or distance.

The stationers, from whom the wedding invitation cards were obtained, will provide the tiny boxes in which to pack the segments of cake. A card, fitting the boxes, should have been printed ready to accompany each piece of cake. The wording will probably be as follows, remembering that the address of the sender will be that of the young couple's new home:

> Mr. & Mrs. Peter J. Himself,
> The Bungalow,
> Esher Meade.

With compliments on the occasion of their wedding.
20th April, 19XX

The bride's maiden name should be printed at top left and crossed through by a silver arrow – and, indeed, all the printing on the card should be in embossed silver.

No acknowledgement of the receipt of the cake should be expected.

On the same day the bride's mother or father can send an announcement of the wedding to the press, for publication in the 'Marriages' section of the classified advertisement columns. (See Chapter 10.)

The local paper is the ideal medium if both the bride and the bridegroom come from the same district; the local paper should be used in each district when the couple come from different parts of the country – and if it should happen that one or other of them was widely known or famous, then publication should be made in one of the national daily newspapers.

The bride's parents must remember that they are expected

to make the announcement – not those of the bridegroom. This should be remembered in the case where the bridegroom lived in a different town to that of his bride. It is still her mother's duty to send the announcement to the paper in that town – though it is quite usual for the bridegroom's mother to undertake the task, by mutual agreement.

And the bride's father must settle down to the task of paying the bills that will flow in to him. He used to be responsible for the cost of the reception, including everything to do with it; the cake, the bridal gown and the bridesmaids' attire, the meal, the wines, the cars, the flowers – while the bridegroom, or his father, needed to square the much smaller account, for the wedding ceremony. Nowadays, many families share the cost more evenly.

A day or so before the newly-weds are due back from their honeymoon, the bride's parents should take all the wedding presents to their daughter's new home.

As soon as possible after they move in, the bride is expected to start on the task of writing to thank all those who gave her and her husband wedding presents, and to acknowledge the greetings messages.

Letters of thanks need to be hand-written; they should neither be printed nor typewritten – however burdensome the duty.

Finally, the last act of the wedding ceremony and ritual takes place spread over the next three months. It is the newly-weds' duty to entertain their relatives and friends in their new home. A few at a time, of course, unless the new home is a very large one. Both sets of parents first – after which priority should go to the best man, the bridesmaids and the ushers, though with them, if there is room in the house, other guests may be added.

Then comes the general run of relatives and friends and their entertainment should be settled as a matter of convenience and preference by the bride and bridegroom. The problem is a matter of the numbers to be invited on each occasion and whether the invitation is to tea, to a cheese and wine party or to dinner.

No mandatory method applies. The couple are at liberty to please themselves – so long as the entertainment is to be in their new house and not outside. On the face of it maiden aunts will prefer to foregather for tea, the friends and relatives of the same generation as the newly-weds to a cheese and wine party and the parents and grandparents perhaps to a dinner.

No formal invitation need be sent out. Verbal arrangements or a brief note is sufficient – and acceptances will be returned in the same manner.

16

CHOICE OF MENU FOR THE RECEPTION – AT HOME OR AWAY

Likes and dislikes are so individual where food and drink is concerned that it is only possible to make a few tentative suggestions within the scope of a book of this nature.

A glance at the tome-like Mrs. Beeton will warn you that the scope is unlimited.

The most important point to consider before deciding on a menu is where the meal is to be cooked and served.

However expert the housewife, it is improbable that her cooking facilities match that of a first class restaurant or hotel. And even if the bride's mother has in mind a menu that can easily be dealt with in her own kitchen, she needs to be highly organised to undertake the cooking and serving of such a meal, as she will be the hostess and should normally never have to leave her guests.

However, it is possible to serve a cold meal which can be prepared in advance, plated and ready to serve from a service table or a sideboard. For instance, if the bride's mother wanted to give a finger buffet she could serve any of the following:

Vol-au-vents
Sausage rolls
Curry puffs
Individual quiches

which need to be popped into the oven for ten minutes or so to warm through.

Fried chicken drumsticks
Cheese and pineapple on cocktail sticks
Sausages on sticks
Thin strips of fried fish served with a dip
Asparagus rolls
Small sandwiches
Profiteroles filled with cream cheese
Small cakes
Choux buns
Biscuits

On the other hand, if she felt she could cater for a fork buffet with three courses, she might start with:

Savoury mousse or
Paté or
Stuffed eggs

followed by:

A whole salmon
Chicken or turkey pieces served in a sauce
Cold sliced ham, tongue, beef or turkey served with salads such as:

Potato salad
Mixed bean salad
Brown rice with corn salad
Celery, walnut and apple salad

and many others which can be found in any good cookery book. 'Salad' no longer has to mean a lettuce leaf and half a tomato!

Fruit salad with cream and meringues

Gateaux
Pavlovas
Éclairs or choux buns
Trifle with cream

followed by tea or coffee.

If the bride's family have called in a caterer they will be offered a choice of menus to fit their purse. A hot meal is only advisable where a hall has adequate kitchen facilities or the caterer does not have a long journey. The following are typical of the choice available:

No. 1
Assorted sandwiches
Filled bridge rolls
Chicken and mushroom vol-au-vents
Sausage rolls
Genoese fancies
Fruit salad and fresh cream
Coffee

No. 2 (fork buffet)
Cold ham and tongue
Veal, ham and egg pie
Potato salad, Russian salad, green salad, tomato salad
Rolls and butter
Sausage rolls, cocktail sausages
Assorted pastries
Fruit salad and fresh cream
Coffee

No. 3 (sit down meal)
Soup or orange and grapefruit cocktail

Rolls and butter
Fillet of Sole Princess
Hot roast chicken with bacon
Buttered new potatoes, garden peas
Fruit salad and cream
Coffee
Petit fours

No. 4 (sit down meal)
Melon cocktail
Smoked salmon with lemon and brown bread
Cold roast turkey with ham, various salads
Croquette or buttered potatoes

alternatively:

Hot roast turkey with stuffing
Buttered or croquette potatoes
Garden peas
Sherry trifle with cream
Cheese board
Petit fours
Coffee

No. 5 (fork buffet)
Lobster or crab mayonnaise
Roast fillet of beef with horseradish sauce
Chicken in cream sauce with pineapple
Served with green salad, rice with peppers
French bread and butter
Lemon soufflé, or chocolate gateau
Coffee

No. 6 (sit down meal for a summer wedding)
Salmon mousse

Roast fillet of beef with English mustard
Prawn mayonnaise
Served with hot new potatoes, green salad, kidney beans,
    carrots, fennel, and chicory in herb vinaigrette salad
Strawberries or raspberries and cream
Coffee

If the reception is to be held at a restaurant or hotel any menu is possible provided the items are available and the hostess is prepared to pay for the meal she envisages. Certainly, hot meals are better in a restaurant or hotel where they have all the facilities on hand and the food can be cooked when required, and not hours beforehand then to be kept warm or re-heated, as can happen in a hired hall.

It is usual to offer the guests a glass of sherry or white hock on their arrival at the reception. Increasingly popular is the use of sparkling wines throughout the reception or a still white wine with a good champagne being used for the toasts. As there are always children at weddings as well as those guests who cannot (or do not wish to) drink anything alcoholic there should always be a good supply of fresh fruit juice, apple and grape juice, or a jug of non-alcoholic fruit punch on each table.

The amount required can be estimated on the basis of six glasses of wine or champagne to each bottle except in the case of German wine where you get five glasses to the bottle, and the average guest having three-four glasses (or half a bottle of wine) each.

Champagne is of course the traditional wedding drink, but there can be no doubt that snob value has had a lot to do with its popularity. The mere fact that it is one of the most expensive wines has given champagne an air of being 'right' for such occasions and springs to mind at once.

With the increase in holidays abroad, more and more people are becoming increasingly knowledgeable about wines, but for those who are not specialists the following ideas may be helpful.

If sherry is to be offered at the beginning of the reception it can either be:

Fino:	Dry
Amontillado:	Medium or
Oloroso:	Sweet (also called 'cream').

At most weddings nowadays it is usual to offer a good sparkling wine such as a French Blanquette de Limoux or a good German Sekt and this would be drunk throughout the reception, including the toasts.

The Italian Asti Spumante and Spanish Cordoniu sparkling wines, while very pleasant, tend to be sweeter and are, therefore, less popular for receptions.

The alternative would be a still white wine such as a dry French white Chablis or Graves or a sweeter German from the Moselle such as Piesporter or Michelsberg, or from the Rhine a Bornheimer or Adelberg. This would be followed by champagne for the toasts. Champagne comes from the two regions around the towns of Rheims and Epernay in France, and can be either vintage or non-vintage. From Rheims you get Bollinger, Krug and Heidsieck champagne and from Epernay, De Castallanne, Pol Roger, and Moet et Chandon. From a good house a non-vintage champagne will be two–three years old, and a vintage champagne will be at least five years old. These houses declare a vintage year when the climate and the crop have been exceptional and it follows that not every year is a vintage year.

For those who like red wine the Rhone offers a very interesting variety of well-priced wines such as Cotes-de-Rhone-Villages, Crozes-hermitage or the magnificent Chateauneuf-du-Pape. These wines are considered to be well-priced alternatives to the Burgundies. There are also the small chateaux wines of Bordeaux.

If the reception is to be at home or in a hall, the local wine shop or off-licence will usually arrange supplies on a sale or return basis and will lend glasses. In a hotel or restaurant, the manager will suggest which wines he has in his cellar and which are the most suitable. They will normally charge for the bottles actually opened.

Champagnes, white wines and sherries should be chilled – two or three hours in cold water will help where no ice or other coolant is available.

Red wines should be served at room temperature by being left on the dining room sideboard for an hour or more before they are to be served.

Bottles of red wine should be uncorked about an hour before being served to allow the contents to 'breathe'.

If more than one wine is to be served, remember that dry white wines should be drunk before both red wines and sweet wines, and that younger wines should always be served before older ones.

17

SILVER AND GOLDEN WEDDINGS

Wedding anniversaries have always been regarded as a purely private occasion between a man and his wife – except on the rare days when the 'silver' or 'golden' weddings come around.

Other than those, the anniversaries are usually celebrated with a private party *a deux*. Perhaps they enjoy themselves for the evening with a dinner followed by a visit to the theatre; maybe a dinner-dance is their choice or a visit to a night club and often an eternity ring to mark the first anniversary.

As the years go by the couple tend to gather about themselves a family and the regular celebrations tend to become a thing of the past. Forgotten perhaps; often made impracticable by the demands of babies.

Even then many couples at least try and mark the day in some small way. An exchange of small presents and perhaps something special for dinner, including a bottle of wine, or a meal out.

And still the years slide past and the couple begin to become so absorbed in a welter of such events as children's birthdays, Christmas Days, the school holidays – and in time, their children's own wedding days, that suddenly, almost unbelievably, they find the day approaching when they have completed a quarter of a century of married life. Their Silver Wedding Day.

Something special is called for. First, an announcement in the press, sent by the couple themselves, might read:

HIMSELF:HERSELF — on 20th April 19XX at St. George's Parish Church, Woodhouse, Peter John Himself to Ann Herself. Present address: The Bungalow, Esher Meade.

Secondly, they will exchange gifts and may expect to receive presents from their family and close friends. Where possible, the presents should consist of silver articles, or where this is not feasible because of cost, particularly gifts from children and grandchildren, the gift should be tied into a parcel with silver ribbon.

The couple may decide to entertain their children and close friends – and wherever possible, the long ago best man and chief bridesmaid, to a small party.

Formal invitations are not necessary, but they should be issued well in advance so that those who are to be invited may be given time to make their own arrangements.

Formal wear is not usual except in families where it is customary to attend and dress for functions – and the numbers should be restricted to about a dozen.

The venue can be a hotel or a restaurant and is generally arranged in advance so that a small, private room may be reserved for the occasion, or more often it is held at home.

A wedding cake usually graces the occasion and, following the meal, it is cut in the same token fashion as applied on the occasion of the wedding itself, twenty-five years earlier.

Speeches are usually few and happy. The eldest son might propose the 'Health and Happiness' of his parents and the husband should reply on behalf of his wife and himself. Other speeches may follow – almost entirely composed of reminiscences – from the best man or one of the guests who was present at the wedding.

The party may go on to a theatre or a dance.

Another quarter of a century may go by and then comes the grand occasion of the Golden Wedding. On this occasion the small party to celebrate the event is usually organised by the eldest son of the couple – often in consultation with his brothers and sisters.

He will make the announcement public through the press, in similar fashion to that published twenty-five years before.

This time the presents should be of gold, though very often they are much less valuable and merely tied up with gold coloured ribbon.

Again, the party can be held at a hotel or restaurant if at all possible and equally, if possible, the guests of twenty-five years previously should be invited once again – together with the rising generation of grandchildren. Often one of the daughters may arrange the party, do the catering, and hold it in her home.

No formal dress is required nor need any official invitations be sent out. A cake is usual though not obligatory.

After the cutting of the cake there may be a few informal speeches – but the husband is not compelled to reply in person. Sometimes the youngest grandson present performs this office for him – though there is no set order of precedence involved.

It is unusual for any sort of entertainment to follow. The guests talk over their coffee and as soon as the old couple begin to show signs of tiring, the eldest son should bring the proceedings to a close.

It is customary for the eldest son and his wife to escort his parents home. They do not stay when they arrive – and none of the guests should follow.

The Diamond Wedding follows on the anniversary of their sixtieth wedding day – and takes very much the same lines as that described as being applicable to a Golden Wedding. However, the presents almost never consist of diamonds and rarely of anything of more intrinsic value than flowers.

The family party should be kept as small as possible and because of the age of the couple, is usually held either in their own home, or that of one of their children.

The wedding cake need only be a token and, as on previous anniversaries, there is no need for pieces of it to be distributed to absent friends and relatives.

The whole celebration must be geared to the ability of the couple to stand up to the fuss – and, again, the elder son and his wife should bring the proceedings to a close as soon as tiredness begins to dull the pleasure of the couple.

As a matter of interest, though of little moment today, anniversaries of a wedding are traditionally known as:

1st anniversary	Cotton
2nd anniversary	Paper
3rd anniversary	Leather
4th anniversary	Silk
5th anniversary	Wood
6th anniversary	Iron
7th anniversary	Wool
8th anniversary	Bronze
9th anniversary	Pottery
10th anniversary	Tin
12th anniversary	Linen
15th anniversary	Crystal
20th anniversary	China
25th anniversary	SILVER
30th anniversary	Pearl or Ivory
35th anniversary	Coral
40th anniversary	Ruby
45th anniversary	Sapphire
50th anniversary	GOLD
55th anniversary	Emerald
60th anniversary	DIAMOND
75th anniversary	and again, DIAMOND

APPENDIX

Marriage fees alter from time to time and the up-to-date position should be checked.

Fees for marriage according to the rites of the Church of England

Fee payable to the Church Authorities for the
   ceremony £36.00
Marriage after Banns
   (i) Fee for publication of Banns £4.50
   (ii) Fee for certificate of Banns £2.50
Marriage by Common Licence
   Fee for licence £28.00
Marriage by Special Licence
   Fee payable at the Faculty Office £50.00
Marriage by Superintendent Registrar's certificate
   For entering a notice of marriage £10.00
   (two notices are required to be given if the
   parties reside in different registration districts)

Fees for marriage in Church otherwise than according to the rites of the Church of England

Marriage by Superintendent Registrar's certificate

(i) For entering a notice of marriage £10.00
(two notices are required to be given if the parties reside in different registration districts)

(ii) For the attendance of a registrar in a register office £12.00

(iii) For the attendance of a registrar in a registered building, where required £21.00

Marriage by Superintendent Registrar's certificate and licence

(i) For entering a notice of marriage £10.00
(ii) For the issue of the licence £28.00
(iii) For the attendance of a registrar in a register office £12.00
(iv) For the attendance of a registrar in a registered building, where required £21.00

Civil fees

Total fees for the preliminaries to marriage by Superintendent Registrar's certificate:

1. If both parties live in the same district:

(a) In the register office £22.00
(b) In a registered building when the presence of a registrar is required £31.00

2. If the parties live in different districts:
(a) In the register office £32.00
(b) In a registered building when the presence of a registrar is required £41.00

Total fees for the preliminaries to marriage by Super-intendent Registrar's licence:

(a) In the register office £50.00
(b) In a registered building when the presence of a
        registrar is required £59.00

Certified copy of the entry of marriage at the time
of registration £2.00

INDEX

BEST MAN'S DUTIES

by Vernon Heaton

The best man is certainly the third most important person at any wedding ceremony. This book is the ideal detailed guide for this most important person.

Includes everything from his duties at the bride-groom's stag party to his role at the service and reception. Also a sample speech in reply to the toast of 'the bridesmaids'.

Brand-new and completely re-written edition now available.

Uniform with this book

ELLIOT RIGHT WAY BOOKS
KINGSWOOD, SURREY, U.K.

SAMPLE SOCIAL SPEECHES

WIT, STORIES, JOKES, ANECDOTES, EPIGRAMS

by Gordon Williams

At last! The book the world has waited for.

Gordon Williams has worked out a technique based on numerous specimen speeches, to enable you to use them to build up your social speech.

He has set out many samples on which you can base a talk or speech of your own. You can add to it with stories from his unique selection, or 'salt' it with one or more of his jokes, epigrams and witticisms.

This new edition includes many more speeches for weddings and similar occasions.

Uniform with this book

ELLIOT RIGHT WAY BOOKS
KINGSWOOD, SURREY, U.K.

OUR PUBLISHING POLICY

HOW WE CHOOSE

Our policy is to consider every deserving manuscript and we can give special editorial help where an author is an authority on his subject but an inexperienced writer. We are rigorously selective in the choice of books we publish. We set the highest standards of editorial quality and accuracy. This means that a *Paperfront* is easy to understand and delightful to read. Where illustrations are necessary to convey points of detail, these are drawn up by a subject specialist artist from our panel.

HOW WE KEEP PRICES LOW

We aim for the big seller. This enables us to order enormous print runs and achieve the lowest price for you. Unfortunately, this means that you will not find in the *Paperfront* list any titles on obscure subjects of minority interest only. These could not be printed in large enough quantities to be sold for the low price at which we offer this series. We sell almost all our *Paperfronts* at the same unit price. This saves a lot of fiddling about in our clerical departments and helps us to give you world-beating value. Under this system, the longer titles are offered at a price which we believe to be unmatched by any publisher in the world.

OUR DISTRIBUTION SYSTEM

Because of the competitive price, and the rapid turnover, *Paperfronts* are possibly the most profitable line a bookseller can handle. They are stocked by the best bookshops all over the world. It may be that your bookseller has run out of stock of a particular title. If so, he can order more from us at any time—we have a fine reputation for "same day" despatch, and we supply any order, however small (even a single copy), to any bookseller who has an account with us. We prefer you to buy from your bookseller, as this reminds him of the strong underlying public demand for *Paperfronts*. Members of the public who live in remote places, or who are housebound, or whose local bookseller is unco-operative, can order direct from us by post.

FREE

If you would like an up-to-date list of all paperfront titles currently available, send a stamped self-addressed envelope to
ELLIOT RIGHT WAY BOOKS, BRIGHTON RD.,
LOWER KINGSWOOD, SURREY, U.K.